THE SPECTATOR BOOK OF EPIGRAMS

Dhiren Bhagat was born in Tokyo in 1957 where his father, an executive in Air India, was stationed. He returned to Bombay as a small boy and was educated at Mayo College in Rajasthan – the equivalent of Harrow or Eton – and at Xavier's College in Bombay.

He came to England to study A Levels before going up to Merton College, Oxford, where, after a false start in Law, he studied Politics, Philosophy and Economics.

He returned to India in 1981 to edit the *New Delhi Review of Books* but the project never got off the ground. He turned instead to journalism, writing for a number of Indian newspapers and periodicals with a fortnightly column in the *Sunday Observer*. His iconoclastic writing led him to be known as the *enfant terrible* of Indian journalism and his reputation was assured when a number of scoops in 1987 and 1988 caused parliament to cross-question the government.

He travelled frequently between London and Bombay and started writing regularly for the *Spectator* with articles on anything from India to the Animal Liberation Front.

In 1986, the *Observer* in London made him its South-East Asia correspondent based in New Delhi. In addition to his journalism, Dhiren published some of his poetry in *Poetry London Apple Magazine* and wrote a number of short stories. He had drawn up a sketch for his first novel, had all but completed *The Spectator Book of Epigrams* and was working on a travelogue of the Punjab when he suffered a fatal car accident in Delhi on 24 November 1988.

GW00383008

A *Poeme* is not alone any worke, or composition
of the Poets in many, or few verses; but even one
alone verse sometimes makes a perfect
Poeme . . .

And anciently, all the Oracles were call'd
Carmina; or, whatever Sentence was express'd,
were it much, or little, it was call'd, an
Epick, Dramatick, Lyrike, Elegiake, or
Epigrammatike Poeme.

Ben Jonson *Timber, or Discoveries* (1640)

The Spectator Book of
EPIGRAMS

EDITED BY
DHIREN BHAGAT

WITH A FOREWORD BY
CHARLES MOORE

PAN BOOKS
LONDON, SYDNEY AND AUCKLAND

First published 1993 by Pan Books Ltd

a division of Pan Macmillan Publishers Limited
Cavaye Place London SW10 9PG
and Basingstoke

Associated companies throughout the world

ISBN 0-330-32547-7

1 3 5 7 9 8 6 4 2

A CIP catalogue record for this book is available from
the British Library

Typeset by Cambridge Composing (UK) Limited, Cambridge
Printed and bound in Great Britain by
Cox & Wyman Ltd, Reading

CONTENTS

FOREWORD

In his introduction, Dhiren Bhagat tells you about the epigram. Let me tell you about Dhiren Bhagat. I laughed when I read his words: 'What is important is that the epigram must pursue a *single* idea and that it is pared of excess.' Dhiren never pursued a single idea, and it would have been terrible if he had tried (though I am sure he would have failed) to pare himself of excess.

Dhiren was an Indian, and an Anglophile, but not one of those irritating Indians who merely ape the English and try to jettison their native land. He was romantic about England, went to Oxford, and visited the country frequently after going down, but he never intended to live here all the time, and he played an increasingly important part in the journalism of his own country. Had he lived, he would undoubtedly have gone far. It was part of his charm that he sometimes went *too* far.

I first met Dhiren by chance in a restaurant in Covent Garden. I was editor of the *Spectator* at the time, and India was on the point of bloodshed over the Sikh problem in the Punjab (later the cause of Mrs Gandhi's assassination). Dhiren told me he had penetrated the Golden Temple in Amritsar and interviewed Bhindranwale, the militant holy man who was occupying it. I asked him to write it up for us, and the result was a terrifyingly vivid picture of the mind of a fanatic. From then on, Dhiren wrote for me irregularly but frequently, and no subject seemed beyond his grasp. At one moment he would be in Hollywood, at the next witnessing a raid on a factory farm by the Animal Liberation Front somewhere in north-west England. He wrote about arranged marriages, and arms deals, and he interviewed statesmen, all with equal aplomb.

I

Some who can tackle so many subjects tend not to write very well, being jacks of all trades and masters of none. But Dhiren did write well because he communicated an immense curiosity about human nature, and because he loved and cared about words. He was extremely well educated and well read, without being fusty. He brought all his learning to bear upon the modern world. It added to his powers of perspective, and it fed his love of the incongruous and the surprising.

That love may explain his taste for epigrams. He liked to see how words could be played with, and used wittily. He liked the ingenious, the scabrous, the worldly. And he enjoyed the hunt for them. Dhiren was a natural anthologist, because he picked up so many shreds and patches from his wide reading and remembered them. His desk was a chaos of quotations scribbled down and fragments photocopied. It is not surprising, perhaps, that this book as originally presented was too long. Dhiren could be relied on to select only what was good, but not to contain his selection to the length prescribed by publishers. His own mind was not, as I say, epigrammatic. We are all grateful to Ross Clark for doing the paring that was required.

The task of editing his own editing did not fall to Dhiren Bhagat, because he died. He had recently moved to Delhi, where his career was prospering. One day in 1988 he drove to the airport there, overtook a lorry on the way, was hit by a lorry coming in the other direction, and was killed instantly. He was only thirty years old. Fortunately, the manuscript of this book was complete. But it is so sad to think of all the great things he did not write, of the many projects which he planned and would have accomplished if he had lived.

This anthology will assist any serious student of the epigram, and delight the more casual reader too. For Dhiren's friends, it gives additional pleasure because the choice bears the stamp of his character. As I browse through it, I conclude that the pleasure will not be confined to his friends: all readers will find disclosed in this selection the engaging personality of a most unusual man.

The book before you comes with the *imprimatur* of the *Spectator*, and that is fitting, because Dhiren Bhagat found in that magazine the fulfilment of his notion of journalism and of English literary life, but the work is all his.

Charles Moore
6 May 1992

INTRODUCTION

No literary form has been more prolific, none more
complex in its development. The bulk of epigrammatic
literature is therefore vast; yet an even more serious
obstacle to the student is the all but total neglect which
the epigram has suffered in literary history. The whole
field represents to the explorer an uncharted jungle.

> Thomas Whipple
> 'Martial and the English Epigram'
> *University of California Publications*
> *in Modern Philology* Vol. 10 (1920)

Epigrams today are suffering from neglect. Many people
regard them as little more than the pastime of puffy aesthetes
who wore green carnations and plied young boys with champagne. Others are loath to think of them as anything more
dignified than sharp doggerel, raillery that rhymes.

Such denunciation is not entirely new. Edward Phillips in
1675 declared the epigram to be 'the fag end of poetry'.
Dryden similarly dismissed it as 'the bottom of all poetry'.
Early in the eighteenth century Addison endeavoured in the
Spectator 'to banish this Gothic Taste which has taken Pos-
session among us'. Lord Chesterfield is recorded as condemn-
ing epigrammatists – even though he was himself the author
of at least four epigrams.

In spite of our general indifference to them, we do in fact
live in one of the greatest periods for the production of epigrams. It is easy to miss this fact, partly because, unlike
blunt Yorkshiremen, poets do not bother to call an epigram
an 'Epigram'. This is unfortunate because it obscures the long
tradition of which such poems are part.

The object of this anthology is to encourage people to read epigrams as epigrams. According to Boswell it was one of Dr Johnson's literary schemes to compile 'A Collection of Epigrams, with Notes and Observations'. Had this been accomplished all might now be well. I have attempted to fill the gap.

There have, of course, been previous attempts at an anthology: I have listed them in the bibliography at the end of this collection. Unfortunately there is little order to be found amongst them. The best is H. P. Dodd's *The Epigrammatists* (1870). It is thorough and accomplished but has the misfortune to have been produced during the Victorian era, when the English epigram was at its most anaemic. Consequently he omitted much valuable material, dismissing it as 'a mass of servility, scurrility, indecency and puerility'. Obviously it does not include the many good epigrams written since 1870.

WHAT IS AN EPIGRAM?

Nothing could be more hopeless than an attempt to discover or derive a definition wide enough to include all the vast multitude of little poems which at one time or other have been honoured with the title of epigrams, and precise enough to exclude all others.

Encyclopaedia Britannica
Eleventh Edition (1919)

This, this, that, that: pointing is perhaps the easiest method of defining the many forms of epigram. Genres change shape as they go along. The label 'epigram' was variously used in Greek and Latin literature and since its entry into the English language has undergone 400 years' worth of perceptible and imperceptible shifts so that, for example, there is little in common between a Jacobean and Victorian epigram.

The first epigrams were inscriptions in metre, the earliest of which appeared on Greek tombstones around the seventh century BC. Written mostly in elegiac couplets, they were short and impersonal. Renaissance theorists attributed these qualities to the lapidary function of epigrams, but it may be a mistake to think this a sufficient explanation. Alistair Fowler has suggested that 'epigrammatists could have composed briefly in order to simulate inscriptions'.

Because the early epigrams eschewed 'point', Greek examples are often described as 'insipid' as shown by this entertaining tale published in *Menagania* in 1716:

> . . . M. de Racan one day went to see Mademoiselle de Gournay, who showed him some epigrams she had written and asked his opinion of them. M. de Racan did not care for them, and said that they lacked point. 'That does not matter at all,' said Mademoiselle de Gournay, 'for these are epigrams *à la Greque*.' Afterwards, they went together to dine at the house of M. de Lorme. Their host having set before them a *potage* which was not very good, Mademoiselle de Gournay turned to M. de Racan and said: 'What a vile soup!' 'Mademoiselle,' replied he, 'it is soup *à la Greque*.' This phrase was repeated so widely that in many circles 'soup *à la Greque* became the usual designation for a tasteless *potage*; and one said of a cook, 'He makes soup *à la Greque*.'

It is not true that all Greek epigrams were devoid of point. Within the *Greek Anthology* – a collection spanning 1600 years – the form keeps changing. Two distinct developments are worth noting. Asklepiades in the early third century BC, and later Kallimachos and the other poets of the Ionian school, used the epigram as a vehicle for personal poetry. With Lucilius and his contemporary Nikarchus in the first century AD it was an occasion for fun: hyperbole and point are the chief qualities of these jesting epigrams that were later to influence the Roman Martial.

Born in Spain in the year AD 40, Martial settled in Rome in

his early twenties. His twelve books of epigrams were written in the age of Pliny, when Latin writers were beginning to explore Greek methods. It was Martial who injected satire into the epigram.

In English these days we tend to describe epigrams as either 'Greek' or 'Roman'. Julius Caesar Scaliger, however, derived a more complex form of classification in his book *Poetices* (1561). He defined five emblematic types: *fel* ('gall'), *acetum* ('vinegar'), *sal* ('salt'), *mel* ('honey'), and *foetidas* ('stinkingness'). He described *mel* epigrams as 'amatory' (which these days might be called 'Greek') and all others 'pointed' (which might now be called 'Roman'). In addition he suggested some epigrams were 'composite'.

The recent history of the English epigram can be seen as an alternation between the two. Doctor Johnson may have amused himself on sleepless nights translating Greek epigrams, but when it came to defining 'epigram' he followed the taste of his time and opted for the Roman model. 'A short poem terminating in a point' reads the succinct entry in his *Dictionary* of 1755. Inevitably, reaction set in. 'The effect of Martial's influence on our epigrammatic literature,' complained a critic in 1870, echoing the learned opinion of the day, 'has been disastrous. The pithy fullness, the elegant simplicity, the graceful turn, the sound sense, the guileless humour and the inoffensive point, which characterized the epigram in its ancient home among the Greeks, has been exchanged for the redundant wordiness, the coarse conceit, the rough satire, the puerile imbecility, the unchaste wit and the stinging point of the Roman school.' Such fretting paid off: the Victorian epigram became elegiac and shed its sharpness.

Almost everyone is agreed on brevity as a condition of the epigram. But this must not be taken too absolutely; it is not a question of two, four, six or eight lines. Martial on occasion wrote poems thirty-two lines long, and we continue to classify these as epigrams. As Martial himself explained: 'things are not long from which you can subtract nothing'. What is important is that the epigram must pursue a *single* idea and that it is pared of excess. Padded poems, however short, are not epigrams.

Moreover, genuine epigrams can be said to consist of two elements, the *Erwartung* ('expectation'), the setting forth of circumstance or incident so as to awaken expectation, and the *Aufschluss* ('explanation'), the conclusion which in some way gratifies or amusingly deceives the expectation.

HISTORY OF THE ENGLISH EPIGRAM

It is to fifteenth-century Florence that we owe the revival of epigrams in Europe. In the 1470s Lorenzo de Medici embarked upon a search for lost classical literature, sending his pupil John Lascaris to the East to collect manuscripts. Aided by Greek scholars who had fled to Florence after the fall of Constantinople in 1453, Lascaris edited the Planudean anthology, which was first printed in 1484. The first Aldine edition of the anthology appeared in Venice in 1503, and soon there was a rush of editions. The other Greek anthology, that of the tenth century Byzantine anthologist Kephalas, was rediscovered in 1606 in the Count Palatine's library at Heidelberg.

Printing made possible the widespread dissemination of literature. The *edito princeps* of Martial appeared in either Venice or Rome in 1471, and from this period there are several undated editions. The first edition of Martial in the vernacular is Clement Marot's posthumously published translation in French (Poitiers, 1547).

The publication of the *Greek Anthology* – an amalgamation of the Planudean and Kephalas' works – was a catalyst to the creation of the neo-Latin epigram. Under its influence, scholars all over Western Europe began to write polished epigrams. Perhaps the most remarkable of these was Sir Thomas More, whose *Epigrammata* (Basel, 1518, 1520) virtually introduced the Greek epigram to England. Almost a third of the epigrams in this book are translations from the *Greek Anthology*.

In 1550 two volumes appeared advertising English epigrams. Robert Crowley's collection *Thirtie One Epigrams* was something of a misnomer: it contained thirty-three longish medieval poems. John Heywood's *An Hundred Epigrammes* was influenced not so much by Martial as by English jest books.

Though Henry Howard, Earl of Surrey, had translated an epigram of Martial's in *Tottel's Miscellany* (1557), the vogue for Martial took some time to establish itself. Timothe Kendall, who translated a number of Martial's epigrams in his *Flowres of Epigrammes* (1577), observed:

> Martial is much mislikt, and lothde,
> of modest mynded men;
> For leude lascivious wanton woorks . . .

One imagines it was a common attitude; Kendall himself omitted the erotica.

There was a fallow period of some fifteen years after the appearance of Kendall's book. The major poets of the day, Sidney and Spenser, did not write epigrams. But the move towards Martial, which Kendall had initiated, continued, notably in the work of Sir John Davies and Sir John Harington. The lyrical element was excluded, the satirical developed. The disillusionment of the last years of the sixteenth century were felt in the poetry.

The Latin tags that served as titles to many of the epigrams of this period suggest they were inspired by exercises performed at schools, where the writing of epigrams had been an established practice since the twelfth century. With the arrival of the *Greek Anthology* this practice flourished. 'And would you ever have believed it,' exclaimed Erasmus in 1528, 'that among the English and the Dutch, schoolboys babble Greek, and exercise themselves, not unhappily, in Greek epigrams?' Kendall and Harington wrote epigrams at Eton; John Owen, Sir John Davies, Thomas Bastard, John Hoskins and John Heath at Winchester. Some went on to teach: Owen, the most popular neo-Latin epigrammatist, was headmaster of Warwick School, and far more famous in his day than Shakespeare. Ben Jonson described him as a 'pure pedantic schoolmaster, sweeping his living from the posteriors of little children'.

Davies (whose epigrams were burned by the public hangman) and Harington (whose other notable achievement was the invention of the flushable lavatory) both developed the English epigram, but much of the court verse of the time was shoddy and imitative, designed to impress not express. C. S. Lewis was particularly strong in his criticism of the epigrams of the 1590s: 'none of them rise so high as mediocrity . . . there is probably not a single epigram which displays as much talent as a good limerick.' Yet epigrams and epigrammatists enjoyed a fame they were never to enjoy again. Thomas Fuller tells the following story of Sir John Harington:

It happened that, while the said Sir John repaired often to an ordinary in Bath, a female attendress at the table, neglecting other gentlemen who sat higher, and were of greater estates, applied herself wholly to him, accommodating him with all necessaries, and preventing his asking anything with her officiousness. She being demanded by him the reason of the careful waiting on him? 'I understand,' said she, 'you are a very witty man: and if I should displease you in anything I fear you would make an epigram of me.'

(*Worthies of England* III 103–4 1840)

She was not alone in her apprehension. In *Return from Parnassus* (1606) Sir Roderick says: 'I hope at length England will be wise enough: I hope as i' faith; then an old knight may have his wench in a corner, without any Satires or Epigrams.'

Ben Jonson, the greatest English epigrammatist, stands beyond fashion. He had a high opinion of the epigram, but his notions were not shared by his contemporaries. Jonson regarded his epigrams as 'the ripest of my studies' and his method of writing 'the old way and true'. Without disavowing Martial he looked to other influences as well. Dekker once accused Jonson of 'wanting the tongue of the epigram', to which he eloquently replied:

> Play-wright me reads, and still my verses damns,
> He says, I want the tongue of Epigrams;
> I have no salt; no bawdrie he doth mean.
> For wittie, in his language, is obscene.

But Jonson had little influence on the writing of epigrams. The fashion for strong lines did not abate: between 1596 and 1620 more than fifty volumes of epigrams were published, and in this period the epigram attracted even more attention than the sonnet. But after 1625 good poets – with the exception of Crashaw and Herrick – ceased to regard epigrams seriously. In 1639 Thomas Bancroft records rather plainly that 'they're out of fashion'.

The epigram is often dismissed by serious people as an aristocratic hobby, a form fit only for the fawning and bitching of courtiers. The poets of the sixteenth century were presumably responsible for this impression but even then there were some who thought epigrams low, even common. Dryden, in the seventeenth century, thought them only suitable for the 'upper gallery audience in a playhouse, who like nothing but the husk and rind of wit; prefer a quibble, a conceit, an epigram before solid sense and elegant expression!' These, he claimed, were the 'mob readers'.

The epigram's scurrilous reputation was capitalized upon in the eighteenth century when political epigrams began to make a greater appearance. Earlier, one ran a considerable risk writing a political epigram – licensing laws made publication difficult. For example, the author of the fifteenth-century satire

> The Cat, the Rat and Lond the Dog
> Rule all England under the Hog

was put to a painful death by Richard III (called a hog because his symbol was a white boar). The Cat (Katesby), the Rat (Sir Richard Ratcliffe) and Lond the Dog (Lovell) were all members of his household.

The most celebrated political epigram of the seventeenth

century, Sir Walter Raleigh's attack on the financial policy of the first Earl of Salisbury, was circulated by word of mouth:

> Here lies Hobinall, our pastor whilere,
> That once in a quarter our fleeces did shear;
> To please us, his cur he kept under clog,
> And was ever after both shepherd and dog;
> For oblation to Pan, his custom was thus,
> He first gave a trifle, then offered up us;
> And through his false worship such power he did gain
> As kept him on the mountain, and us on the plain.

It is not the most accomplished of verses, yet it had a sensational effect at the time and it could not have made Raleigh's life very secure: King James I said he hoped its author would die before he did.

A century and a half later there was more such political sniping from non-aristocrat authors. In 1769 was published *The Patriotic Miscellany. Being a collection of interesting papers, jests, anecdotes, epigrams &c in the case of John Wilkes, Esq.*; 1794 saw the publication of a little book called *Tom Paine's Jests*, containing a number of epigrams. And from *A Genuine Collection of the several pieces of Political Intelligence Extraordinary* I quote this fairly typical extempore 'On the Report of the Death of Mr John Wilkes, in exile in Paris':

> When Wilkes! A Name to Patriots ever dear!
> (Ye sons of Freedom! drop a grateful Tear!)
> First heard that P – t Apostate was become,
> He trembled for his country's fatal doom.
> Grief stopt the current of Blood He tried
> To stem the dreadful shock in vain – and died.

Pitt was a favourite target in the eighteenth century. In particular, his decision to take a peerage and become the Earl of Chatham provoked many a radical epigram. In the newspapers of the day 'Tom Thorne' and 'Sam Sly' were prolific, though today we are more likely to wince at their puns than their politics:

> Now corn is shipp'd to foreign shores, 'tis plain
> Even PITT at will can be a ROGUE IN GRAIN.
>
> 'Sam Sly'

On the evening of 12 February 1793 William Pitt the Younger and Dundas had been drinking heavily at the latter's house on the west side of Wimbledon Common. By the time the two reached the Commons the pleasures of dessert caused them to stagger. What made this behaviour so remarkable was the occasion – the acceptance of the French Declaration of War. Pitt tried to speak and was pulled down by friends when his inability to do so became obvious. Dundas wisely remained silent but a third party spread the story. A Professor Porson who heard about the incident sat up all night and turned out 101 epigrams, none of which, it must be said, did his scholarship much credit. They were published in the *Morning Chronicle* and became the subject of much gossip. The best ones were:

> In what old ways we taste misfortune's cup –
> While France throws *down* the gauntlet, Pitt throws *up*.

> 'Who's up?' inquired Burke of a friend at the door:
> 'Oh! no one,' says Paddy; 'though Pitt's *on the floor*.'

The eighteenth century obsession with 'point' at the expense of all other poetic qualities, and its preference for puns, was to prove debilitating for the epigram. Equally unfortunate was the development of an obsession with sincerity – until many epigrams became simply pompous.

The emphasis on sincerity came, of course, with Wordsworth, the only Poet Laureate never to have written a line as part of his duties. (The only official poem written during his tenure was composed by his son-in-law Edward Quillinan and passed off as his.) In the 'Essays on Epitaphs' (1810) sincerity is introduced as a serious criterion for the first time ever in English criticism. The poet, it was said, must be emotionally involved with the subject of the epitaph; insincerity 'shocks the moral sense'. Commenting on the eighteenth-century epitaphs in *Elegant Extracts* (1784) Wordsworth observes 'there is scarcely one which is not thoroughly tainted by the artifices which have overrun our writings in metre since the days of Dryden and Pope. Energy, stillness, grandeur, tenderness . . . all these are abandoned for their opposite, – as if our Countrymen, through successive generations, had lost the sense of solemnity and pensiveness . . .'

The Greek epigram was subsequently revived, and dozens of volumes of translations from the *Anthology* appeared on the market. Dodd noted this with relish, pithily remarking: 'Supply will follow demand.' What followed was not a golden age for the epigram, although it produced Walter Savage Landor, one of our finest epigrammatists.

The epigram suffered much in the hands of the Victorians. They produced pale elegiac works and they produced mechanical, comic writings – fatuous jokes without sting or wit. There was little in between. 'We seem to have lost the art of writing epigrams,' observed the anonymous author of *All the Year Round* in 1870. 'The art of the epigram is a lost art,' complained *Chamber's Journal* twelve years later. In 1899 the *Spectator* spoke of 'the incapacity for epigram which may be said to characterize our modern world'.

What the Victorians lacked in inspiration they made up for in perspiration. They developed something of an anthology industry. There was Booth (1863), Reeve (1866), Palmer (1869), Dodd (1870), Carey (1872), Tegg (1875), Cheales (1877), Standring (1877) and Adams (1879): nine in the space of sixteen years. But the narrow Victorian sense of propriety had so sanitized and disinfected the contents of these that a reviewer in the *Times Literary Supplement* was later to remark:

English good nature – 'a virtue so peculiar to you,' as Clarendon said when trying to persuade his compatriots to forget the bitternesses of the Civil War, 'that it can be translated into no other language, hardly practised by any other people' – has prevented the making of barbed arrows of obloquy such as are common in the French language.

The scope of the epigram has broadened considerably over the last 100 years. Most important of all there has been a degentrification of the genre since Mortimer Collins wrote the following in *Belgravia* (vol. 14) in 1871:

> Expect no epigrams from the man who earns his bread by the gray goosequill. They don't pay . . . Peers of the realm, country gentlemen, deans of cathedral chapters and fellows of colleges are your natural epigrammatists – if only they have the genius. The epigram should be matured in a lofty library with windows looking to the sunset, shut in from all rude sounds of the outer world; with a plate of filberts and a glass of old madeira or port to occupy the intervals of thought.

Since the turn of the century the modernist taste for minimalist forms of expression has brought the epigram back into fashion – although many twentieth-century epigrams are not recognized as such and are simply called 'poems'. Short, pithy and succinct, the epigram is ideally suited to the contracted concentration spans of our age.

Some of the best poets of our time have managed to combine in their work the strengths of both Greek and Roman models: the reverberating quality of the best Greek epigrams with the earthiness of the Roman. It is not a new achievement but a rare one: Ben Jonson, our finest epigrammatist, achieved it; and so, less evenly, did Herrick. In a recent translation of *Palladas* Tony Harrison combines the two types to form a thumping yet marvellously open-ended epigram:

> Think of your conception, you'll soon forget
> What Plato puffs you up with, all that
> 'immortality' and 'divine life' stuff.

Man why dost thou think of Heaven? Nay
Consider thine origin in common clay

's one way of putting it but not blunt enough.
Think of your father, sweating, drooling, drunk,
you, his spark of lust, his spurt of spunk.

Harrison isn't the only one: Peter Porter, Howard Nemerov, J. V. Cunningham, Andrew Harvey, Alistair Elliot . . . without the madeira or the filberts a revival has taken place. Yet when literary historians look back at the second half of the twentieth century what will amaze them is how indifferent the reading public has been to this achievement.

A NOTE ON ANTHOLOGISTS

Some folk gather bones and rags
From other people's rubbish bags:
Then, when they have got enough
Of the miscellaneous stuff,
They peddle round the rag and bone
Fancying it's all their own.
                    Martin Armstrong *54 Conceits* (1933)

Scholars will probably complain that my classification of epigrams is arbitrary, that the tricksy chapter headings are neither mutually exclusive nor collectively exhaustive. They would be right in the complaint but wrong to complain. The aim of this book is not to satisfy taxonomists but to be read. My classification is convenient rather than methodological.

There is one more exercise of editorial authority that may appear arbitrary: in this collection I have not included those epigrams that are instances of recognizable humorous forms.

17

Limericks, clerihews, double dactyls and the like: these may or may not be epigrams. In recent years, however, entire anthologies have been devoted to these forms and they are, in consequence, too well known to require special pleading.

Dhiren Bhagat

ACADEMICAL

THE UNAPT NOT TO BE
FORCED TO LEARNING

To Salamanca if thou send an Ass,
to Oxford, Cambridge, Paris, or Douai,
or that by travel to farthest lands he pass,
or in the princes' court long time do stay:
if, when he went, he were an Ass, no art
will make him horse, for field, for way, for cart.

Then spare your cost, if nature give not wit,
to send your sons unto the learned schools,
for to the same, if nature make not fit,
do what you can, they still shall prove but fools;
then turn each wit to that which nature will,
else fondly throw thy son and cost dost spill.

Francis Thynne   *Emblemes and Epigrames* (1600)

OF THE SMALL RESPECT HAD OF
LEARNED MEN IN GENERAL

Caligula, envying the bright fames
Of Homer, Virgil and grave Livius,
O'erthrew their statues, to o'erthrow their names.
But would these times had none more barbarous!
For in this age Caligulas we find
That let them starve that shine in either kind.

John Davies of Hereford   *Wit's Bedlam* (1617)

OF IMPUDENT LYNUS

Not any learning, Lynus, no, God knows,
But thy brute boldness made some to suppose,
That thou might'st have been bred in Brazen-nose.
A murren on thy pate, 'twould do thee grace,
   So were thine head so arm'd in every place,
   As Steel skull, Copper nose, and a Brazen face.

Sir John Harington
The Most Elegant and Wittie Epigrams (1618)

WHO MOST MAD?

Nice scholars are most mad, that fight & sweat
Only 'bout vowels, and for sound and air.

Edward May   *Epigrams Divine and Morall* (1633)

A VERY THIN METAPHYSICIAN

Scarce from Privation's dreary lap,
   Thy shadowy form drawn forth we see;
A scanty shred; a tiny scrap
   Of metaphysic entity!

Thy face, in hieroglyphic style,
   Seems just mark'd out; thy waist a span:
Thou sketch! thou out-line! thou profile!
   Thou bas-relievo of a man!

Richard Graves   *Euphrosyne* (1776)

EXPERTO CREDITE*

No wonder that Oxford and Cambridge profound
In learning and science so greatly abound,
When all carry thither a little each day,
And we meet with so few who bring any away.

Anon   *Morning Chronicle* (7 August 1809)

ON DR JOWETT, FELLOW OF ST JOHN'S

A *little* garden *little* Jowett made,
And fenced it with a little palisade;
A *little* taste hath *little* Doctor Jowett;
This *little* garden doth a *little* show it.

Richard Porson   Watson, *Life of Richard Porson* (1861)

ON BENJAMIN JOWETT,
MASTER OF BALLIOL

First come I. My name is Jowett.
There's no knowledge but I know it.
I am Master of this College,
What I don't know isn't knowledge.

H. C. Beeching   *The Masque of B-ll--l* (1881)

* Believe me who know.

ON SOLOMON LAZARUS LEE, EXHIBITIONER OF BALLIOL

I am featly-tripping Lee,
Learned in modern history,
My gown, the wonder of beholders
Hangs like a foot-note from my shoulders.

H. C. Beeching   *The Masque of B-ll--l* (1881)

MR SIDNEY WEBB

Strange paradox his fair repute entombs –
The politician of the Common Rooms,
Turned, in a Cabinet ,where the unlettered shone,
Exemplar of the cobweb-strangled Don.

Hubert Phillips   *A Diet of Crisps* (1929)

GNOME

Spend the years of learning squandering
Courage for the years of wandering
Through a world politely turning
From the loutishness of learning.

Samuel Beckett   written 1934 *Collected Poems* (1977)

A SCHOOLMASTER

A pompous rigmarole he takes for life,
Correcting exercises, caning bums.
He took the blackboard death to be his wife
And left a brood of sodomites and sums!

Roy Campbell   *Mithraic Emblems* (1936)

ACADEMIC

The stethoscope tells what everyone fears:
You're likely to go on living for years,
With a nurse-maid waddle and a shop-girl simper,
And the style of your prose growing limper and limper.

Theodore Roethke   *Open House* (1941)

AMATORIAL

OF LOVE

And if Love be Lord, who or what is he?
If Love be not, who then bereaves my rest?
If no such thing, alas what aileth me?
What breeds such broil, what wounds my yielding breast?
  To tell what tis, doth pass my knowledge far,
  But who so loves I see doth live in war.

Thomas Howell *Devises* (1581)

AMOR CAECUS*

Love through our eyes doth first an entrance find,
How is it then they say love is blind?
Know ye not how both these may well agree?
Though he be blind, yet can his mother see.

John Heath *Two Centuries of Epigrams* (1610)

* Love is Blind

24

VENUS

Love comes and goes, retires, returns,
   As Seas do ebb and flow,
How come it Love's so like the Sea?
   How? Venus thence did grow.
In Venus is Variety,
   Sometimes She Nill, She Will;
Therefore with Moving-Planets plac'd,
   Not with Stars standing still.

John Vicars   *Epigrams of John Owen* (1619)

ON A GENTLEWOMAN,
WORKING BY AN HOUR-GLASS

Do but consider this small dust,
   Here running in the Glass,
   By Atoms mov'd:
Would you believe that it the body was
   Of one that lov'd?
And in his Mistress flames, playing like a Fly,
Was turned into Cinders by her eye?
Yes; as in life, so in their deaths unblest:
A Lovers ashes never can find rest.

Ben Jonson   *Execration Against Vulcan &c* (1640)

TO HIS MISTRESS

Sweetest fair be not too cruel,
Blot not beauty with disdain,
Let not those bright eyes add fuel
To a burning heart in vain,
Lest men justly when I die
Deem you the candle, me the fly.

Anon   *Witt's Recreations* (1640)

TO SAPHO

Sapho, I will choose to go
Where the Northern winds do blow
Endless Ice, and endless Snow:
Rather then I once wo'd see,
But a winters face in thee,
To benumb my hopes and me.

Robert Herrick *Hesperides* (1648)

A MARIGOLD

Now to the set, now to the rise, I turn;
Have I not sense? In the Sun's love I burn.

James Wright   *Sales Epigrammatum* (1663)
From the Latin of Benedictus Jovius

For what To-morrow shall disclose,
May spoil what You To-night propose:
England may change; or Cloe stray:
Love and Life are for Today.

Matthew Prior   *Poems on Several Occasions* (1718)

ON A LADY WHO COULD COMMAND HER TEARS

Why Chloe, why this voluntary tear?
No, Mistress, such spontaneous throbs endear.
Should I the beauty of your form admire,
Such ready streamings would but quench the fire.
Could frequent floodings make a briny sea,
You think you should another Venus be.
Leave Chloe, leave your dewy cheeks to wet,
Thence Venus rises, there, alas! you set.
A fruitless hope your sickly fancy feeds,
Love's not an insect, that in moisture breeds.
Tho' his bright mother did in ocean thrive,
Yet little Cupid has not learnt to dive.

Anon   *The British Apollo* (1740)

ON A GENTLEMAN'S JOSTLING A PRETTY LADY IN SNOWY WEATHER

Pardon me, Chloris, nor my rudeness blame,
I little thought a frost cou'd breed a flame;
But now I burn and rage in strong desires,
And melt like flakes of snow with sudden fires.
    Had you been black, I cou'd have shun'd the flow,
    For diff'rent colours will each other show,
    But you are cold, and fair, and ev'ry way like snow.

Anon   *The British Apollo* (1740)

Whisp'ring close a maid, long courted,
Thus, cry'd Drone, by touch transported;
Prithee, tell me gentle Dolly!
Is not loving long a folly?
Yes, said she, with smile reproving,
Loving long, and only loving.

Aaron Hill   *Works* (1753)

Great goose the painter was, upon my word,
Who Cupid first portrayed with wings. A bird
He knew perchance to paint, but 'tis great odds
His skill forsook him when he sketched the Gods.

Nor light is Love, but far the heaviest ill,
Nor doth he fly at all, or ever will,
Depart when entertained, but firmly clings.
How can a creature of this sort have wings?

Richard Garnett   *Idylls and Epigrams* (1869)

TO A JILT

Girl, when rejecting me you never guessed
I gave you all the beauty you possessed.
Now that I've ceased to love you, you remain
As once, a creature singularly plain.

Martin Armstrong   *54 Conceits* (1933)

EVEN AS THE HEART

Even as the heart – how stark the cost! –
May grieve that it grieves no more, in vain,
So love, its inmost impulse lost,
    Dies never to rise again.

Walter de la Mare   *Complete Poems* (1969)

A STATUE OF EROS

Who carved Love
    and placed him by
this fountain,
    thinking
he could control
    such fire
with water?

Peter Jay   *The Greek Anthology* (1973)
After the Greek of Zenodotus

If someone's with her, then
I'll go, but if she sleeps
alone please let me in,
and say that drunk I came
past brigands to this door,
and bold love guided me.

Edward Lucie-Smith   *The Well-Wishers* (1974)
From the Greek of Posidippus

The blacksmith's quite a logical man
to melt an Eros down and turn
the God of Love into a frying pan,
something that can also burn.

Tony Harrison   *Palladas: Poems* (1975)
After the Greek of Palladas

I wrote, she never replied:
That goes on the debit side.
And yet I'm sure she read it:
That I put down as credit.

James Michie   *Martial: The Epigrams* (1978)

AUTHORIAL

IN MACRUM

Thou canst not speak yet Macer, for to speak
Is to distinguish sounds significant.
Thou with harsh noise the air dost rudely break,
But what thou utterest commonsense doth want:
   Half English words, with fustian terms among
Much like the burthen of a Northen song.

        Sir John Davies   *Epigrammes and Elegies* (159–?)

OF A RAILING HUMOUR

(Good Lord!) that men should have such kennel wits
To think so well of a scald railing vain,
Which soon is vented in beslavered writs.
As when the cholic in the guts doth strain
   With civil conflicts in the same embrac't
   But let a fart, and then the worst is past.

        Everard Guilpin   *Skialetheia* (1598)

Be not aggrieved, my humourous lines afford
   Of looser language here and there a word,
Who undertake to sweep a common sink,
   I cannot blame him, though his bosom stink.

        Henry Peacham   *The More the Merrier* (1608)

AD TE (SCABIOSA POETA)*

Scalpo hath got an itch in Poetry,
With which conceit doth oft his elbow scratch,
And sooner hopes to come in print hereby,
Than any younger beginner of his match:
    As cast off Chamber-maids convert to Drabs,
    So may thy itch in time break out in scabs.

Henry Parrot   *Laquei Ridiculosi* (1613)

FATALES POETAE

Witches and Poets coimbrace like fate
Reputed base, bare, poor, unfortunate,
In these respects, I may myself intrude
Among the Poet's thickest multitude.

Henry Parrot   *Cures for the Itch* (1626)

OF BARDUS

Bardus complaineth of such thievish men
As in their writings made use of his pen;
Be patient Bardus, 'tis young Scholars use,
If they want pens to go and plume a Goose.

John Pyne   *Epigrammata Officiosa, Religiosa, Iocosa* (1627)

* To You, Scabby Poet

(ON BEAUMONT'S EARLY DEATH)

He that hath such acuteness and such wit,
As would ask ten good heads to husband it;
He, that can write so well that no one dare
Refuse it for the best, let him beware:
    Beaumont is dead, by whose sole death appears,
    Wit's a disease consumes men in few years.

Richard Corbet   written c. 1628 *The Epigrammatists* (1870)

TO SOME GREAT ONES

Poets are great Mens Trumpets, Poets fein,
Create them Virtues, but dare hint no stain:
This makes the Fiction constant, and does shew
You make the Poets, not the Poets you.

Charles Cotton   *Poems on Several Occasions* (1689)

TO NISUS

How shall we please this Age? If in a Song
We put above six lines, they count it long;
If we contract it to an Epigram,
As deep the dwarfish Poetry they damn;
If we write Plays, few see above an Act,
And those lewd Masks, or noisy Fops distract:
Let us write Satire then, and at our ease
Vex th'ill natur'd Fools we cannot please.

Sir Charles Sedley   *Poetical Works* (1710)

AN EPIGRAM ON THE SPECTATOR

When first the Tatler to a Mute was turn'd,
Great-Britain for her Censor's Silence mourn'd;
Robb'd of his sprightly Beams, she wept the Night
Till the Spectator rose, and blaz'd as Bright.

So the first Man, the Sun's first setting view'd,
And sigh'd, till circling Day his Joys renew'd;
Yet doubtful how that second Sun to name,
Whether a Bright Successor, or the Same.

So we – but Now from this Suspense are freed,
Since all must own, who both with Judgement read,
'Tis the same Sun, and does Himself succeed.

Nahum Tate   *An Epigram on the* Spectator (1712)

APOLLO'S REVENGE ON DAPHNE,
MORE FAMILIARLY

In merry old England it once was a Rule,
The King had his Poet, and also his Fool:
But now we're so frugal, I'd have you to know it,
That C---R can serve both for Fool and for Poet.

Anon   *Certain Epigrams in Laud
and Praise of the Gentlemen of the Dunciad* (1732)

I am no genius, you affirm: and why?
Because my verses please by brevity.
But you, who twice ten ponderous volumes write
Of mighty battles, are a man of might.
Like Prior's bust, my work is neat, but small:
Yours like the dirty giants in Guildhall.

William Hay   *Select Epigrams of Martial* (1755)
After the Latin of Martial

Scribbletonius, thy volumes, when'er we peruse,
    This idea they always instil; –
That you pilfer'd, felonious, the brains of a goose,
    When you robb'd the poor bird of a quill!

Anon   *An Asylum for Fugitive Pieces* (1785)

MR C------Y'S APOLOGY

FOR KNOCKING OUT A BOOKSELLER'S TEETH, WHO TOLD HIM THAT HIS WORKS WOULD NOT SELL

I must confess that I was somewhat warm,
When I broke D——y's teeth; but where's the harm?
My work, he said, would ne'er afford him meat,
And teeth are useless where there's nought to eat.

Anon   *The Poetical Farrago* (1794)

THE POET'S POWER

True poets can depress and raise,
Are lords of infamy and praise;
They are not scurrilous in satire,
Nor will in panegyric flatter.

Unjustly poets we asperse;
Truth shines the brighter clad in verse;
And all the fictions they pursue
Do but insinuate what's true.

Jonathan Swift (?)   *The Poetical Farrago* (1794)

LINES TO A REVIEWER

Alas, good friend, what profit can you see
In hating such a hateless thing as me?
There is no sport in hate where all the rage
Is on one side : in vain would you assuage
Your frowns upon an unresisting smile,
In which not even contempt lurks to beguile
Your heart, by some faint sympathy of hate.
Oh, conquer what you cannot satiate!
For to your passion I am far more coy
Than ever yet was coldest maid or boy
In winter noon. Of your antipathy
If I am the Narcissus, you are free
To pine into a sound with hating me.

Percy Bysshe Shelley
Leigh Hunt, *The Literary Pocket-Book* (1823)

Night comes; with Night comes Silence, hand in hand;
With Night comes Silence, and with that, Repose;
And pillows on her drowsy breast and locks
Within the marble prison of her arms
The Poet's rash and feverish melancholy;
Cuts short the feignings of fantastic grief,
Freezes the false breath on the parted lips,
And steals the shallow music of his tongue.

Matthew Arnold   written c. 1844 *Yale MS*

Ten thousand flakes about my windows blow,
Some falling and some rising, but all snow.
Scribblers and statesmen! are ye not just so?

Walter Savage Landor   *Works* (1846)

Poet! I like not mealy fruit; give me
Freshness and crispness and solidity;
Apples are none the better overripe,
And prime buck-venison I prefer to tripe.

Walter Savage Landor   *Last Fruit* (1853)

A CRITIC

With much ado you fail to tell
The requisites for writing well;
But what bad writing is, you quite
Have proved by every line you write.

Walter Savage Landor   *Dry Sticks* (1858)

Fired with the thirst of Fame, thus honest Sam,
'I will arise and write an epigram.'
An epic, Sam, more glorious still would be,
And much more easily achieved by thee.

Richard Garnett *Idylls and Epigrams* (1869)

Old tips come out as good as new
From me, for I am M–NT–GUE;
With head aslant I softly cram
The world into an epigram.

J. W. Mackail *The Masque of B–ll--l* (1881)

TO A POET, WHO WOULD HAVE ME PRAISE CERTAIN BAD POETS, IMITATORS OF HIS AND MINE

You say as I have often given tongue
In praise of what another's said or sung,
'Twere politic to do the like by these;
But was there ever dog that praised his fleas?

W. B. Yeats *The Green Helmet and Other Poems* (1910)

GEORGE MOORE

Women he praised and, after women, Art.
Good friends he had, and used them all for copy.
Had but his genius matched as great a heart,
Time had not mixed his laurels with the poppy.

Humbert Wolfe *Lampoons* (1925)

MR BELLOC

Our faith, our strategy, our dance and song –
There's nothing, it would seem, but's going wrong;
And, what is worse, with each successive blow
He keeps on shouting that he told us so.

Hubert Phillips   *A Diet of Crisps* (1929)

CUTTLEFISH'S BOOKS

Those who call Cuttlefish The Coming Man
Say, '*He can write*' – I do not doubt he can;
I dare say, also, he can read and spell,
Do sums not badly, and spin tops quite well.

Colin Ellis   *Mournful Numbers* (1932)

ADDER'S EPIGRAMS

Adder, whose art condenses and refines
The value of three volumes in two lines,
Is still dissatisfied, and racks his head
To say things better that were best not said.

Colin Ellis   *Mournful Numbers* (1932)

REVIEWERS

People with a turn for spite
Write about what others write,
And their still more spiteful brothers
Write on those who write on others.
Lord who rulest sea and land
Save us from the secondhand.

Martin Armstrong   *54 Conceits* (1933)

THE SPUR

You think it horrible that lust and rage
Should dance attention upon my old age;
They were not such a plague when I was young;
What else have I to spur me into song?

W. B. Yeats   *Last Poems* (1939)

WHERE ARE THE WAR POETS?

They who in folly or mere greed
Enslaved religion, markets, laws,
Borrow our language now and bid
Us to speak up in freedom's cause.

It is the logic of our times,
No subject for immortal verse –
That we who lived by honest dreams
Defend the bad against the worse.

Cecil Day Lewis   *Word Over All* (1943)

'POEMS FOR SPAIN'

No sooner had its sales begun
Than all the reds were on the run
And only halted (sink or swim!)
To hack each other limb from limb –
So, once at least beneath the sun
Poetic Justice has been done!

Roy Campbell   *Talking Bronco* (1946)

POINTS OF VIEW

This Satirist, well-meaning, makes a hubbub
In scorn of the benighted in a suburb;
And they, poor happy naturals, persist
In blissful ignorance of the Satirist.

Walter de la Mare   *Spectator* (19 September 1952)

A POET'S EPITAPH

They call you 'drunk with words'; but when we drink
And fetch it up, we sluice it down the sink.
You should have stuck to spewing beer, not ink.

Kingsley Amis   *A Case of Samples* (1956)

A SACRIFICED AUTHOR

Father, he cried, after the critics' chewing
Forgive them, for they know not what I'm doing.

Howard Nemerov   *The Next Room of the Dream* (1962)

VOICE FROM THE TOMB

NIGHTMARE, AFTER READING THE
PARABLE OF THE TALENTS

Here lies a poet who would not write
His soul runs screaming through the night
Oh give me paper, give me pen,
And I will very soon begin.

Poor Soul, keep silent; in Death's clime
There's no pen, paper, notion,
And no Time.

Stevie Smith   *The Frog Prince and Other Poems* (1966)

A QUESTION OF VALUES

Christopher Marlowe or Francis Bacon
   The author of *Lear* remains unshaken.
Willie Herbert or Mary Fitton
   What does it matter? The Sonnets were written.

Noël Coward   *Not Yet The Dodo* (1967)

CLERICAL

OF CINNA

Five years hath Cinna studied Genesis
And knows not yet what *in Principio* is
And griev'd that he is graveld thus, he skips,
O'er all the Bible, th'Apocalypse.

Sir John Harington
The Most Elegant and Wittie Epigrams (1618)

IN SACRIFICUM QUANDAM*

A Priest for Penance, one enjoined to take
A journey with three peas, loose in his shoe:
Which he, devoutly given, did not forsake,
But fram'd himself his Penance straight to do:
   Yet, that he might perform it with more ease,
   His wit did serve him, first to boil the peas.

John Ashmore   *Certaine Selected Odes* (1621)

* On a Certain Priest

UPON GLASS

Glass, out of deep, and out of desp'rate want,
Turn'd from a Papist here, a Predicant.
A Vicarage at last Tom Glass got here,
Just upon five and thirty pounds a year.
Add to that thirty five, but five pounds more,
He'll turn a Papist, ranker than before.

Robert Herrick   *Hesperides* (1648)

UPON BLOOD'S ATTEMPT
TO STEAL THE CROWN

When daring Blood, his rents to have regain'd,
Upon the English diadem distrain'd,
He chose the cassock, surcingle, and gown
(No mask so fit for one that robs a crown),
But his lay-pity underneath prevail'd,
And while he spar'd the Keeper's life, he fail'd.
With the priest's vestments had he but put on
A bishop's cruelty, the crown was gone.

Andrew Marvell
*The Second Part of the Collection
of Poems on Affairs of State* (1689)

(SPOKEN EXTEMPORE TO A COUNTRY CLERK AFTER HAVING HEARD HIM SING PSALMS)

Sternhold and Hopkins had great qualms
When they translated David's psalms
   To make the heart full glad;
But had it been poor David's fate
To hear thee sing, and them translate,
   By God! 'twould have made him mad.

John Wilmot, Earl of Rochester
Workes of Rochester and Roscommon 3rd edn (1709)

When e'er I meet you, still you cry,
What shall I do with Bob, my boy.
Since this affair you'll have me treat on,
Ne'er send the lad to Paul's or Eton.
The Muses let him not confide in,
But leave those Jilts to Tate or Dryden.
If, with damn'd Rhymes he racks his Wits,
Send him to Mevis or St Kit's.
Would you with Wealth his Pockets store well,
Teach him to pimp, or hold a door well.
If he has a head not worth a Stiver,
Make him a curate, or Hog-driver.

Thomas Brown   *Works* (1715)
After the Latin of Martial

SHALL I REPINE

If neither brass nor marble can withstand
The mortal force of Time's destructive hand
If mountains sink to vales, if cities die
And lessening rivers mourn their fountains dry
When my old cassock, says a Welsh divine
Is out at elbows, why should I repine?

Jonathan Swift   *The Holyhead Journal* (1727)

ON SEEING A WORTHY PRELATE GO OUT OF CHURCH IN THE TIME OF DIVINE SERVICE, TO WAIT ON HIS GRACE THE DUKE OF DORSET

Lord Pam in the Church (cou'd you think it) kneel'd down,
When told the Lieutenant was just come to Town,
His Station despising, unaw'd by the Place,
He flies from his God, to attend on his Grace:
To the Court it was fitter to pay his Devotion,
Since God had no Hand in his Lordship's Promotion.

Jonathan Swift   *Miscellanies, Vol. the Third* (1732)

Against our Bishops Henley raves,
    Tho' all allow they're useful Tools;
The Viscount in like sort behaves,
    And calls our Statesmen bungling Fools.

But now suppose his Majesty
    (I wish he wou'd but try it)
Shou'd offer Henley some rich see,
    D'ye think he wou'd deny it?

The Viscount too wou'd soon be blind
  If taken into Favour
For naught like Golden Chains can bind
  A Man to Good Behaviour.

Anon   *The Honey Suckle* (1734)

(WRITTEN IN IMITATION
OF A GREEK EPIGRAM)

When hungry Wolves had Trespass'd on the Fold,
And the robb'd Shepherd his sad Story told;
'Call in Alcides,' said a crafty Priest,
'Give Him One half and He'll Secure the rest.'
No, said the Shepherd, if the Fates decree
By ravaging my Flock to ruin me,
To their Commands I willingly resign;
Pow'r is Their Character, and Patience mine:
Tho' troth to me there seems but little Odds,
Who prove the greatest Robbers, Wolves or Gods?

Matthew Prior   Drift, *Miscellaneous Works* (1740)

ON READING THAT THIRTY PRAYER-BOOKS
WERE STOLEN OUT OF A CHAPEL

Thirty Prayer-Books to steal, was a bad speculation,
  Since long by the thief they may lie;
For Piety now is a drug in the nation,
  That few will be willing to buy.

Anon   *A Collection of Poems, Epigrams etc.*
Extracted from Newspapers (1770–95?)

A QUARRELSOME BISHOP

To hide her ordure, claws the cat;
You claw, but not to cover that.
Be decenter, and learn at least
One lesson from the cleanlier beast.

Walter Savage Landor   *Last Fruit* (1853)

Here lies a Doctor of Divinity;
    He was a Fellow too of Trinity:
He knew as much about Divinity,
    As other Fellows do of Trinity.

Richard Porson   Watson, *Life of Richard Porson* (1861)

(EPITAPH FOR REVD. I. SQUIRES)

In earlier life I freely shed my blood
Both for my country and my country's good
In later life it was my pride to be
Soldier to him who shed his blood for me.

Swansea
Anon   *Epigrams and Epitaphs* (1877)

FELLOW SUFFERERS

A Bishop in his pastoral charge
Declared his palace over large:
To some poor outcasts I could name
The Thames Embankment seems the same.

Charles Dalmon   *Singing As I Go* (1927)

48

LIVING ON SIN

The hasty sin of the young after a dance
Awkward in clothes against a wall or crick-necked
In car, gives many a nun her tidy bed,
Full board and laundrette. God-fearing State
Provides three pounds a week, our conscience money,
For every infant severed from the breast.

Austin Clarke   *Flight to Africa* (1963)

CIRCUMSCRIPTURE

As Pastor X steps out of bed
    He slips a neat disguise on:
that halo round his priestly head
    is really his horizon.

Piet Hein   *Grooks* (1966)

ON MONKS

Solitaries? I wonder whether
real solitaries live together?

Crowds of recluses? Pseuds,
pooling all their 'solitudes'.

Tony Harrison   *Palladas: Poems* (1975)
After the Greek of Palladas

FATAL

OF THE MOTHER THAT ATE HER CHILD
AT THE SEIGE OF JERUSALEM

In doubtful breast, whilst motherly pity
With furious famine standeth at debate,
Saith the Hebrew mother: 'O child unhappy,
Return the blood where thou hadst milk of late.
Yield me those limbs that I made unto thee,
And enter there where thou wert generate.
For of one body against all nature
To another must I make sepulture.'

Sir Thomas Wyatt   Tottel, *Songs and Sonnets* (1557)

OF WAILING FOR THE DEAD

What profiteth to wail the dead,
   and strike myself with pain,
A man may weep till heart strings break,
   Yet have not them again.

Mathew Grove
The Most Famous and Tragical Histories &c (1587)

Ficus was fat in body and in purse,
And unto sea is gone himself to purge,
Some fifteen hundred marks he did disburse,
To receive three for one, a tempting scourge,
To whip my gallant up the surging seas,
And dance to Venice with a whistling wind,
There to evacuate for stomachs ease,
The home–bred crudities his flesh did bind,
Of him we have not heard unto this day,
That I believe he's purged all away.

John Cooke   *Epigrames, Served out in 52 Several Dishes* (c. 1604)

IN OBITUM PROMI*

That Death should thus from hence our Butler catch
Into my mind it cannot quickly sink,
Sure Death came thirsty to the Buttry Hatch,
When he (that busy was) denied him drink:
Tut 'twas not so : 'tis like he gave him liquor,
And Death made drunk, took him away the quicker.
    Yet let not others grieve too much in mind,
    (The Butler gone) the keys are left behind.

Henry Parrot   *Laquei Ridiculosi* (1613)

* On the Death of a Butler

DURUM TELUM NECESSITAS*

Coquus with hunger, penniless constrain'd,
To call for meat and wine three Shillings cost,
Had suddenly this project entertained,
In stead of *What's to pay*, to call mine host;
Who, being come, intreateth him discuss,
What price the law allots for shedding blood,
Whereto mine Host directly answers thus,
T'was always forty pence, he understood.
  So then (quoth Coquus) *to requite your pains,*
  Pray break my head, and give me what remains.

Henry Parrot   *Laquei Ridiculosi* (1613)

MORTIFICATION

We live to die, and die to live: O why,
Then learn we not to die, before we die?

Thomas Harvey   *John Owen's Latine Epigrams* (1617)
From the Latin of Owen

HUMANA FRAGILITAS†

The famous Father Austin doth declare
Glass not to be so brittle as men are:
That last's a World of days, if let alone,
Man of himself decays, and soon is gone.

John Pyne   *Epigrammata Officiosa, Religiosa, Iocosa* (1627)

* Necessity is a hard weapon
† Human Fragility

FATUM SUPREMUM*

All buildings are but monuments of death,
All clothes but winding sheets for our last knell,
All dainty fattings for the worms beneath,
All curious music, but our passing bell;
 Thus death is nobly waited on, for why?
 All that we have is but deaths livery.

       Anon *Witt's Recreations* (1640)

ON SIR F. VERE

Death meeting him arm'd with his sword and shield,
Death was afraid to meet him in the field,
But when his weapons he had laid aside,
Death (like a coward) struck him, and he dy'd.

       Anon *Wit's Interpreter* (1655)

AN EXTEMPORE EPIGRAM ON DEATH

If Death does come as soon as Breath departs,
Then he must often die, who often farts.
And if to die, be but to lose one's Breath,
Then Death's a Fart, and so a Fart for Death.

       Thomas Brown *Works* (1715)

     * The Supreme Fate

When Bibo thought fit from the World to retreat,
As full of Champagne as an Egg's full of Meat,
He wak'd in the Boat, and to Charon he said,
He wou'd be set back for he was not yet Dead:
Trim the Boat and sit quiet, stern Charon reply'd,
You may have forgot, You was Drunk when You Dy'd.

Matthew Prior   Drift, *Miscellaneous Works* (1740)

EPIGRAM ON THE AIR BALLOON

The land alone suffered of yore
    To glut pale Death's destructive train;
Next mid the waves was felt his power
    And now he rules th' aerial plain.
Mankind to surer ruin run.
    Death has three realms instead of one.

Anon   *The Arno Miscellany* (1784)
Translated from the Latin epigram that
appeared in the *Florence Gazette*

TIT FOR TAT

Old Time kills us all,
Rich, poor, great, and small,
    And 'tis therefore we rack our invention;
Throughout all our days,
In finding out ways,
    To kill him by way of prevention.

Anon   *A Select Collection of Epigrams* (1796)

ON INVALIDS

Far happier are the dead, methinks, than they
Who look for death, and fear it every day.

William Cowper Haley, *Life and Letters* (1803)
From the Greek of Lucilius

ON DEATH

On death, tho' wit is oft display'd,
No epigram could e'er be made;
Poets stop short, and lose their breath,
When coming to the point of death.

Anon   *The Cambridge Tart* (1823)

Death stands above me, whispering low
I know not what into my ear:
Of his strange language all I know
Is, there is not a word of fear.

Walter Savage Landor   *Last Fruit* (1853)

Ah, make the most of what we yet may spend,
Before we too into the Dust descend;
Dust into Dust, and under Dust, to lie,
Sans Wine, sans Song, sans Singer, and – sans End.

Edward FitzGerald   *The Rubáiyát of Omar Khayyám*
1st edn (1859)

Strange is it not? that of the myriads who
Before us passed the door of Darkness through,
  Not one returns to tell us of the Road,
Which to discover we must travel too.

> Edward FitzGerald   *Rubáiyát of Omar Khayyám*
> 2nd edn (1868)

A Death blow is a Life blow to Some
Who till they died, did not alive become –
Who had they lived, had died but when
They died, Vitality begun.

> Emily Dickinson   written c. 1864 *Poems by Emily Dickinson*
> Second Series (1891)

A sad and great evil is the expectation of death –
And there are also the inane expenses of the funeral;
Let us therefore cease from pitying the dead
For after death there comes no other calamity.

> Ezra Pound   *Cathay* (1915)
> After the Greek of Palladas

The angler rose, he took his rod,
He kneeled and made his prayers to God.
The living God sat overhead:
The angler tripped, the eels were fed.

> Robert Louis Stevenson
> *Poems . . . Hitherto unpublished* (1916)

Good creatures, do you love your lives
    And have you ears for sense?
Here is a knife like other knives,
    That cost me eighteen pence.

I need but stick it in my heart
    And down will come the sky,
And earth's foundations will depart
    And all you folk will die.

A. E. Housman   *More Poems* (1936)

This is the first thing
I have understood:
Time is an echo of an axe
Within a wood.

Philip Larkin   *The North Ship* (1945)

Does Charidas lie beneath you? If you mean
The son of Arimmas of Kyrene – yes.
Charidas, what's it like down there? Great darkness.
And resurrection? A lie. *And Pluto?*
A fable. *Then we are finished . . .* What I'm saying
Is the truth. If you want to hear something pleasant,
The cost of living is very low in Hades.

Peter Jay   *The Greek Anthology* (1973)
After the Greek of Kallimachos

ANTIC

With a shrug and a sotto 'I'm sorry',
Death to be sure takes off
All who are good and true.
But – pin on his medals
And orders – he
Takes off the others too.

Geoffrey Grigson   *The Cornish Dancer* (1982)

GASTRONOMICAL

A PRISONER

In prison, a prisoner condemned to die,
And for execution waiting daily,
In his hands for worms looking on a day,
Smiling to himself these words did say:
Since my four quarters in four quarters shall stand,
Why harm I these seely worms, eating my hand?
Nought else in this deed do I, but myself show
Enemy to the worm and friend to the crow.

John Heywood   *An Hundred Epigrammes* (1550)

AGAINST APICIUS

Thy tongue Apicius taunnteth none,
  by it no man is stung:
Yet porringers and platters both,
  complain still of thy tongue.

Timothe Kendall   *Flowres of Epigrammes* (1577)
After the Latin of Martial

THE PEACOCK

Thou wondrest when he spreads abroad,
  his wings that glittering look:
And canst thou find in heart, to give
  him to the cruel cook?

Timothe Kendall *Flowres of Epigrammes* (1577)
After the Latin of Martial

THE RAM

With Butchers knife thou carved hast,
  the Ram his tender throat:
Deserved he thus which unto thee
  so often gave his coat?

Timothe Kendall *Flowres of Epigrammes* (1577)
After the Latin of Martial

THE LIAR

Thou in the fields walkst out thy supping hours,
  And yet thou swear'st thou hast supp'd like a king:
Like Nebuchadnezar perchance with grass and flowers,
  A sallad worse than Spanish dieting.

John Donne
written c.1600 Simeon, *Unpublished Poems* (1856–7)

UPON GUESS

Guess cuts his shoes, and limping, goes about
To have men think he's troubled with the Gout:
But 'tis no Gout (believe it) but hard Beer,
Whose acrimonious humour bites him here.

Robert Herrick   *Hesperides* (1648)

ON THE DRUNKARD'S LAVISHNESS

I'll tell you why the drunk so lavish are,
They have too much, nay more than they can bear.

Robert Heath   *Clarastella* (1650)

VINEGAR

Aegyptian Vinegar despise not thou
When it was wine, 'twas far more vile than now.

James Wright   *Sales Epigrammatum* (1663)
From the Latin of Martial

Come, Let's Drink, and drown all sorrow,
  'Tis what the Time invites us to,
And who knows whether tomorrow
  Was ordained for us or no!
    Death watches us, and when that Slave
    Has once enclos'd us in the Grave,
      And heaps of Mold upon us hurl'd;
    Farewell good Victuals and good Wine;
    I read in no Author of mine
      Of Taverns in the other world.

Charles Cotton   *Poems on Several Occasions* (1689)
            After the French of Maynard

THE LONDON VINTNER'S
ANSWER TO MR BROWN

If what thou asserts, dear Thomas, be true,
It is to get rid of such Chapmen as you,
That I and my Brethren have learned to Brew.

Whatever Ingredients are put in the Vat,
Whether Dogs-turd or Honey, no matter for that
For all our design's but to poison a Rat.

He that dies by bad Wine, and not by the Halter
Departs without Chime of Hopkins' Psalter,
And that you well know is no matter of laughter.

Thomas Brown   *Works* (1708)

ON PASSING THROUGH A WINE-CELLAR

Through the Red Sea, on foot, of old, we read,
How Moses did the fav'rite Hebrews lead.
What Deed to brag of, Moses? even we
Have pass'd a redder, and more potent Sea.
Then so much more our courage was than thine;
Thy Sea was Water, but our Sea was Wine.

Anon   *The Honey Suckle* (1734)

ON FASTING

A FRENCH GENTLEMAN DINING WITH SOME COMPANY ON
A FAST-DAY, CALLED FOR SOME BACON AND EGGS. THE
REST WERE VERY ANGRY, AND REPROVED HIM FOR SO
HEINOUS A SIN : WHEREUPON HE WROTE THE FOLLOWING
LINES, EXTEMPORE, WHICH ARE HERE TRANSLATED.

Who can believe with common Sense,
A Bacon-slice gives Good Offence?
Or, how a Herring hath a Charm
Almighty Anger to disarm?
Wrapt up in Majesty divine,
Does he regard on what we dine?

Jonathan Swift   *Miscellanies, Vol. the Fifth* (1735)
From the French

EPITAPH ON JENNY THE FISH

The Waters bore me, next the Earth did Share,
My Life, I now am mounted in the Air:
Through three Elements already past,
It will be well, if I escape the last.

John Winstanley   *Poems* (1742)

One night, Duke Drain-all from his bed,
Flush'd with his usual dose of red,
Into a gallon punch-bowl vents
His throbbing bladder's vast contents.

Wond'rous to tell – the ready bowl
Precisely held, and mark'd the whole:
Four bottles it return'd complete,
And prov'd the wine merchant no cheat.

N. B. Halhed
Imitations of some of the Epigrams of Martial (1794)

WINE VERSUS TEA

If wine be poison, so is tea – but in another shape;
What matter whether we are killed by cannister or grape?

Anon   *The Wild Garland* (1866)

NATURAL SELECTION

'The elephant, landed at Liverpool last Sunday, followed
his conductor into a tavern and spontaneously emptied a
pot of beer' *Weekly Paper*

> Resolve me, glib zealots, agog to uprear
> The banner inflated with honour of beer:
> Can rational folk any longer be neuter? –
> Instinctive Sagacity seizes the pewter!

> Anon   *Epigrams and Other Short Excursions
> by a Cripple of Long Standing* (1869)

POUILLY 1915

> Pouilly, I vow, is Madame la Marquise,
>   And when she enters let no wooer speak
> But watch, with apprehension and unease
>   That faint flush of dominion on her cheek.

> Christopher Morley   *Epigrams in a Cellar* (1927)

from ANNOTATIONS OF AUSCHWITZ

> London is full of chickens on electric spits,
>   Cooking in windows where the public pass.
> This, say the chickens, is their Auschwitz
>   And all poultry eaters are psychopaths.

> Peter Porter   *Once Bitten, Twice Bitten* (1961)

Old Brandy in the heated spoon
Looked dignified at first, but soon
Went off his head and, lost to shame,
Lay wallowing in a fit of flame.

W. H. Auden   *About the House* (1966)

A REMARKABLE THING

A remarkable thing about wine,
which we drunkards and lechers all bless so,
is the way it makes girls look more fine –
but ourselves, on the contrary, less so.

Gavin Ewart   *All My Little Ones* (1978)

LEGAL

IUSTITIA UNIVERSALIS*

An universal, as such, in no case,
Is to be tied to terms of time or place.
Justice is universal, wherefore then,
Seek we now for to find it amongst men?

John Heath   *Two Centuries of Epigrams* (1610)

Two wooers for a wench were each at strife,
Which should enjoy her to his wedded wife:
Quoth th'one, she's mine, because I first her saw,
She's mine, quoth th'other, by Pye-corner law;
  Where sticking once a Prick on what you buy
  It's then your own, which no man must deny.

Henry Parrot   *Laquei Ridiculosi* (1613)

* Universal Justice

FACILE PARTA, FACILIUS LOCATA★

Two lawyers opposite in two men's cases,
Rail'd at each other in most vehement sort,
With many bitter terms and foul disgraces,
As those that heard them, blusht at such report:
   Next night they meeting, laught at their past-jar
   And what they got, spent freely at the Bar.

                 Henry Parrot   *Laquei Ridiculosi* (1613)

A Woman to a Lawyer came, Sir, quoth she
Beseech you do a favour unto me.
What wouldst thou have, the man a law replies?
O sir your helping hand, the good wife cries,
For god sake sir, quoth she, let me entreat
You'll make my husband's small thing very great.
   They say of nothing lawyers can great matters make
   Therefore I pray sir this thing undertake.

            William Goddard   *A Neaste of Waspes* (1615)

★ Easily shared, more easily found.

A PRETTY QUESTION OF LAZARUS
SOUL WELL ANSWERED

Once on occasion two good friends of mine
Did meet at meat, a Lawyer and Divine:
Both having eaten well to help digestion,
To this Divine, the Lawyer put this question:
When Lazarus in grave four days did stay,
Where was his soul? in heaven, or hell I pray?
Was it in hell? Thence no redemption is.
And if in heaven: would Christ abate his bliss?
Sir, said the Preacher, for a short digression,
First, answer me one point, in your profession:
If so his heirs and he had fallen to strife,
Whose was the land, if he came back to life?
   This latter question mov'd them all to laughter,
   And so they drunk one to another after.

Sir John Harington
The Most Elegant and Wittie Epigrams (1618)

OF SOME LAWYERS

Law serves to keep disordered men in *aw*,
But *Aw* preserves orders, and keeps the *Law*.
Were *Aw* away L(AW)YERS would LYERS be
For lucre which they have and hold in Fee.

John Pyne   *Epigrammata Officiosa, Religiosa, Iocosa* (1627)

To what serve Laws where only Money reigns?
Or when a poor man's cause no right obtains?
Even those that most austerity pretend,
Hire out their Tongues, and words for profit lend.
What's Judgement then? but public merchandise;
And the Court sits but to allow the Price.

Henry King   *Bodleian, MS Malone 22* (c. 1640)
After the Latin of Petronius

A QUESTION ABOUT LAW

One ask'd why th'Law was now so much neglected!
Marry (said I) it never was respected,
But still declin'd e'er since the Judges ruffs
Were turn'd to little falling bands and cuffs.

Robert Heath   *Clarastella* (1650)

WHY JUSTICE IS PAINTED BLIND

Who painted Justice blind did not declare
What Magistrates should be, but what they are;
Not so much 'cause they rich and poor should weigh
In their just scales alike; but because they
Now blind with bribes are grown so weak of sight,
They'll sooner *feel* a cause than *see* it right.

Robert Heath   *Clarastella* (1650)

If (as the scripture, in plain terms, records)
We must account for all our idle Words;
How will the lawyers answer when they come
At the Last Judgement, to receive their doom?
For all their needless long Tau-to-lo-gies
Will then, as Evidence, against 'em rise.

Anon   *The Honey Suckle* (1734)

THE LAME AND THE BLIND DISPUTING THE RIGHT TO AN OYSTER FOUND;

THE LAWYER DECIDES THE CONTROVERSY.

Blind Plaintif, Lame Defendent share
The Friendly Laws impartial Care,
A Shell for Him a Shell for Thee
The Middle is the Lawyers Fee.

Matthew Prior   Drift, *Miscellaneous Works* (1740)

THE LAWYER AND CLIENT

Two lawyers, where a knotty cause was o'er
Shook hands, and were as friendly as before:
'Zounds!' said the client, 'I would fain know how
You can be friends, who were such foes just now?' –
'Thou fool!' said one; 'we lawyers, though so keen,
Like shears, ne'er cut ourselves but what's between!'

Anon   *Morning Herald* (22 November 1813)

71

INQUEST – NOT EXTRAORDINARY

Great Bulwer's works fell on Miss Basbleu's head,
And in a moment, lo! the maid was dead!
A jury sat, and found the verdict plain –
'She died of *milk and water on the brain*.'

Anon   *The Jest Book* (1864)

THE INQUEST

Poor Peter Pike is drowned, and neighbours say,
'The jury mean to sit on him today.'
'Knowst thou what for?' said Tom. Quoth Ned, 'No doubt,
'Tis merely done to squeeze the water out.'

Anon   *The Wild Garland* (1866)

MATRIMONIAL

The wicked reap what other men do sow,
But Cuckolds are excepted (that you know).

Henry Parrot   *The Mous-Trap* (1606)

PARI INGO DULCIS TRACTUS*

Wil and his wife so well love one another,
As oft their strife is which would first be dead;
Meanwhile (the better to partake with other)
Lie closely kissing all day long in bed:
  For so their fancies both jump on the nick,
  He calls her *Cunny*, she him *little Prick*.

Henry Parrot   *Laquei Ridiculosi* (1613)

ON OLD COLT

For all night-sins with others' wives, unknown,
Colt now doth daily penance in his own.

Ben Jonson   *Workes* (1616)

* Under one yoke things are sweet.

73

AGAINST THE NOBLY-DESCENDED MUSCUS, WHO WEDDED A BUTCHER'S FAT DAUGHTER

The well-born Muscus wedded hath of late
A Butcher's daughter fat, for pounds & plate:
Which match is like a pudding, sith in that
He puts the blood, her father all the fat.

John Davies of Hereford   *Wit's Bedlam* (1617)

ANTIQUARY

If in his Study he hath so much care
To hang all old strange things, let his wife beware.

John Donne   *Poems* (1633)

UPON BATT

Batt he gets children, not for love to rear 'em;
But out of hope his wife might die to bear 'em.

Robert Herrick   *Hesperides* (1648)

UPON JOLLY AND JILLY

Jolly and Jilly, bite and scratch all day,
But yet get children (as the neighbours say).
The reason is, though all the day they fight,
They cling and close, some minutes of the night.

Robert Herrick   *Hesperides* (1648)

74

OF TITUS

Titus was tame when single; yet since he
Was yok'd in Wedlock, butts most cruelly.

James Wright   *Sales Epigrammatum* (1663)

ON A LITTLE WOMAN'S
MARRYING A LARGE MAN

She hugs her Dear, his Beard she strokes;
Thus Ivy twines the sturdy Oaks.

Anon   *Martial Reviv'd* (1725)

MERULUS & MERULA

Thrice happy Merulus and his wife
The honour of the married life;
He's always feeling of her Bubby
She tickles in return, his Toby;
They shew such Fondness in the Light,
I fear, there's Nothing done at Night.

Anon   *The Scarborough Miscellany for 1734*

EPIGRAM ON THIS QUESTION:

'WHICH IS THE MOST ELIGIBLE FOR A WIFE;
A WIDOW, OR AN OLD MAID?'

'Ye who to wed the sweetest wife would try
'Observe how men a sweet Cremona buy!
'New violins they seek not from the trade,
'But one on which some good musician play'd:
'Strings never try'd some harshness will produce,
'The Fiddle's harmony improves by use.'

'One rule will Wives and Fiddlers fit,
'Is falsely said, I fear, by Wit,
  'To sad Experience blind:
'For Woman's an Æolian harp,
'Whose every note, or flat or sharp,
  'Depends upon the wind.'

Anon   *A Collection of Poems, Epigrams, etc.*
Extracted From Newspapers (1770–95?)

TO THE REVD. DR O---, ON HIS LATE MARRIAGE WITH MISS P--, A LADY OF FORTY-FIVE

My Puritan jolly,
How could you have Dolly?
Sure, sure, you were under a cross spell,
  To be thus trepann'd,
  To cultivate land,
More tough and more hard than the gospel.

Anon   *Garrick's Jests* (1785)

When a Man has married a Wife he finds out whether
Her knees & elbows are only glued together.

William Blake   *Notebook* c.1793

ON MODERN MARRIAGES

When Phoebus was am'rous, and long'd to be rude,
Miss Daphne cried Pish! and ran swift to the wood;
And, rather to do such a naughty affair,
Became a fine laurel to deck a god's hair.
The nymph was, no doubt, of a cold constitution,
For sure to turn tree was an odd resolution!
Yet in this she behav'd like a true modern spouse,
And she fled from his arms to distinguish his brows.

Captain Thompson(?)   *The Merry Companion* (1811)

EPITAPH

Here rest, who never quarrell'd in their lives,
The best of husbands, and the best of wives.
And yet, sad fate! it chanc'd one summer tide,
When in a gig this couple took a ride,
That they FELL OUT – unhappily – and died.

Thomas Dunbar   *The Epigrammatique Garlande* (1818)

POOR MAN'S MARRIAGE

A poor man's marriage,
    Is a dog's fight,
Starts in the morning,
    And lasts all night.

Laurence Dakin
Lyrics and Epigrams from the Greek Anthology (1969)
From the Greek of Callicter

THE COMMON WISDOM

Their marriage is a good one. In our eyes
What makes a marriage good? Well, that the tether
Fray but not break, and that they stay together.
One should be watching while the other dies.

Howard Nemerov   *The Western Approaches* (1975)

MEDICAL

IN CARUM

When Carus died these were the last he spake,
O friends take heed Tobacco was my death.
You that can judge tell me for Carus sake,
He which died so, died he for want of breath?
If so he did, then am I more in doubt
How breath being taken in, may blow breath out?

Thomas Bastard   *Chrestoleros* (1598)

TO DOCTOR EMPIRIC

When men a dangerous disease did 'scape
Of old, they gave a cock to Aesculape.
Let me give two, that doubly am got free
From my disease's danger, and from thee.

Ben Jonson   *Workes* (1616)

A PROGNOSTIC

As many Laws and Lawyers do express
Nought but a Kingdoms ill-affectedness:
Ev'n so, those streets and houses do but show
Store of diseases, where Physicians flow.

Robert Herrick   *Hesperides* (1648)

UPON LEECH

Leech boasts, he has a Pill, that can alone,
With speed give sick men their salvation:
'Tis strange, his Father long time has been ill,
And credits Physic, yet not trusts his Pill:
And why? he knows he must of Cure despair,
Who makes the sly Physician his Heir.

Robert Herrick   *Hesperides* (1648)

IN A WINDOW IN LORD V.........s HOUSE

In Vain by Drugs and rules of Art
    Poor Ratcliff wou'd my Lungs ensure
They lie too near a wounded heart
    Whose sickness Death alone can cure.

Matthew Prior   written 1696 Waller, *Dialogues &c* (1907)

THE REMEDY, WORSE THAN THE DISEASE

I sent for Radcliff, was so ill,
    That other Doctors gave me over,
He felt my pulse, prescribed his Pill
    And I was likely to recover.

But when the wit began to wheeze,
　　And Wine had warmed the Politician,
Cur'd yesterday of my Disease,
　　I died last night of my Physician.

Matthew Prior
Poems on Several Occasions Vol. III 2nd edn (1727)

ON A GENTLEMAN WHO RAN MAD WITH LOVE OF A PHYSICIAN'S DAUGHTER

Employ'd to cure a love distracted swain,
The boasted aid of hellebore is Vain;
None but the Fair the storm she raised can calm;
Her smiles the cordial, and her tears the balm:
In Cynthia's bosom dwells the magic pow'r,
Sov'reign to heal, and vital to restore:
But oh! what medicine e'er could reach the heart?
The daughter's eyes have foil'd the father's art:
For, matchless were the learn'd Physician's skill,
If he could save as fast as she can kill.

George Jeffreys　*Miscellanies in Verse and Prose* (1756)

TO DR SCHOMBERG, OF BATH

To Schomberg quoth Death, 'I your patient will have';
To Death replied Schomberg, 'My patient I'll save.'
Then Death seiz'd his arrow, the Doctor his pen,
And each wound the one gave, t'other heal'd it again;
'Till Death swore he never had met such defiance,
Since he and the College had been in alliance.

Paul Whitehead　*Poems and Miscellaneous Compositions* (1777)

REPENTANCE

Bolus, whom conscience makes afraid,
To follow a less murd'rous trade
   Resolves; so quits his jars,
His gallipots, his draughts, and pills,
His lotions, potions, bark, and squills,
   And lists in the hussars.

J. & H. L. Hunt   *Fables and Epigrams* (1825)
From the German of Lessing

ON A GENERAL PRACTITIONER

WHO DIED SHORTLY AFTER GETTING A SCOTCH DIPLOMA

A son of the pestle, just dubbed an M. D.,
Full vain of his title, wig, ruffles, and fee,
Danc'd off to this place ere his skill could delight us,
By an order from Death, and the dancing St Vitus!

William Wadd   *Nugae Canorae* (1827)

'I DO REMEMBER AN APOTHECARY' *Shakespeare*

O cruel death! you make us very sad,
So soon to take this Pharmaceutical lad.
We should not thus bewail the fatal doom,
Could we but place an equal in his room.

William Wadd   *Nugae Canorae* (1827)

MORAL

OF DISSEMBLING WORDS

Throughout the world, if it were sought,
Fair words enough a man shall find:
They be good cheap, they cost right nought,
Their substance is but only wind.
But well to say and so to mean,
That sweet accord is seldom seen.

Sir Thomas Wyatt   Tottel, *Songs and Sonnetes* (1557)

OF TONGUE, MOUTH, TEETH, AND WISDOM

The tongue is assigned, of words to be sorter:
The mouth is assigned, to be the tongue's daughter:
The teeth are assigned, to be the tongue's porter.
But wisdom is 'signed to tie the tongue shorter.

John Heywood   *Workes* (1562)

83

India new found the Christian faith doth hold,
Rejoicing in our heavenly merchandise,
Which we have chang'd for precious stones & gold
And pearl and feathers, and for popingyes.
Now are they loving, meek and virtuous,
Contented, sweetly with poor godliness.
Now we are savage, fierce and barbarous,
Rich with the fuel of all wickedness.
   So did Elijah's servant Gehazye,
   With Naamans gold, buy Naamans leprosy.

          Thomas Bastard   *Chrestoleros* (1598)

IN SOLEM OCCIDENTEM*

Oft did I wonder why the setting Sun
Should look upon us with a blushing face:
Is't not for shame of what he hath seen done,
Whilst in our hemisphere he ran his race?

       John Heath   *Two Centuries of Epigrams* (1610)

* On the Setting Sun

AGAINST LUCIA'S VARIETY

Fair Lucia's full of Fortune's favours, which
Makes her so wanton proud, she'll fall I fear;
(That's common to the young, if fair and rich)
Now plays she with her dog, then with her deer;
Now here she is, then there, now sits, then dies;
Now sighs, then laughs, and now and then (beside)
She for mere love of alteration, cries;
Because no one thing long, she can abide:
   Then things must needs be short and sweet that she
   Loves long, yet long in love she cannot be,
   Because she only loves variety.

John Davies of Hereford   *The Scourge of Folly* (1611)

TO MY BOOKE

It will be looked for, book, when some but see
   Thy title, *Epigrams*, and named of me,
Thou shouldst be bold, licentious, full of gall,
   Wormwood and sulphur, sharp and toothed withal;
Become a petulant thing, hurl ink and wit
   As madmen stones, not caring whom they hit.
Deceive their malice who could wish it so.
   And by thy wiser temper let men know
Thou are not covetous of least self-fame
   Made from the hazard of another's shame;
Much less with lewd, profane and beastly phrase,
   To catch the world's loose laughter or vain gaze.
He that departs with his own honesty
   For vulgar praise, doth it too dearly buy.

Ben Jonson   *Workes* (1616)

OF CLAUDIA

Claudia, to save a noble Roman's blood,
Was offered by some friends that wisht his good,
A jewel of inestimable price.
But she would not be won by this device:
   For she did take his head, and leave the jewel.
   Was Claudia now more covetous, or cruel?

Sir John Harington
The Most Elegant and Wittie Epigrams (1618)

TO LOGISTA

Though guilty, yet in fault he will not be,
And why? *Lo*: I'm not in fault, the fault's in me;
He's taken in the fact, and yet denies,
His Will did act (for who his heart espies)
And yet he is not freed against his will,
His heart and hand, do therefore both act ill.

Joseph Martyn   *New Epigrams* (1623)

COLORES AETHEREI

The Heav'n sometimes seems to be Red in hue,
In cloudy weather Black, in clearer Blue
The Air such colours to our Sense affords,
Being beate and wounded with blasphemous words.

John Pyne   *Epigrammata Officiosa, Religiosa Iocosa* (1627)

TO A COVETOUS CHURL

Although thy blood be frozen, and thy scalp
Exceed the whiteness of the snowy Alp,
Though thy few teeth can hardly chew the crumb,
Though to the Stygian lake thou now art come,
And though one leg is now within the grave,
Yet still more gold thou dost desire to have:
What dost thou mean? Know Charon does not care
For all thy wealth, one penny is his fare.

Edward May   *Epigrams Divine and Morall* (1633)

TO A TELL-TALE

Thy glowing ears, to hot contention bent,
Are not unlike red Herrings, broil'd in Lent.

Thomas Bancroft
Two Bookes of Epigrammes and Epitaphs (1639)

ON A VIRTUOUS TALKER

If virtue's always on thy mouth, how can
It ere have time to reach thy heart fond man?

Anon   *Witt's Recreations* (1640)

IN HOW FAR MEN ARE INFERIOR TO MANY OTHER LIVING CREATURES, IN THE FACULTIES OF THE EXTERIOR SENSES

In touching, Spiders are the subtlest:
The Bears, in hearing: Vultures, in the smell:
In seeing, Eagles, and the Apes in taste:
Thus beasts in all the senses men excel;
  So that, if men were not judicious creatures:
  Some brutes could be of more accomplish'd natures.

Sir Thomas Urquhart   *Epigrams, Divine and Moral* (1641)

EXPENSES EXHAUST

Live with a thrifty, not a needy Fate;
Small shots paid often, waste a vast estate.

Robert Herrick   *Hesperides* (1648)

NOTHING FREE-COST

Nothing comes Free-cost here; Jove will not let
His gifts go from him; if not bought with sweat.

Robert Herrick   *Hesperides* (1648)

(ON THE SNUFF OF A CANDLE THE NIGHT BEFORE HE DIED)

Cowards fear to Die, but Courage Stout,
Rather than Live in Snuff, will be put out.

Sir Walter Raleigh   Camden, *Remains* (1651)

ON A CERTAIN ENCOMIAST OF VIRTUE

No wonder virtue comes not near thy heart,
When from thy tongue it never doth depart.

James Wright   *Sales Epigrammatum* (1663)
From the Latin of Georgius Benedictus

Oh, England. Sick in head and sick in heart,
Sick in whole and every part,
And yet sicker thou art still
For thinking, that thou art not ill.

Anon   *Bodley M. S. Rawl Poet. 66* (1675–1700?)

AN EPIGRAM ON TANTALUS

Unhappy, Tantalus, amidst the Flood,
Where floating Apples on the surface stood,
Ever pursu'd them with a longing Eye,
Yet could not Thirst nor Hunger satisfy.
Such is the Miser's Fate, who curst with Wealth,
In midst of endless Treasures starves himself.

Anon   W. Cavendish, *The Charms of Liberty &c* (1709)

To John I ow'd great Obligation;
But John, unhappily, thought fit
To publish it to all the Nation:
Sure John and I are more than quit.

Matthew Prior   *Poems on Several Occasions* (1718)

ON JESTING

Among the follies that discourse infest,
I count the passion for perpetual jest.
Grant the Jest good : his judgement were not nice,
Who still should load your plate with Salt and Spice.

James Fordyce   *Poems* (1786)

He who binds to himself a joy
Does the winged life destroy
But he who kisses the joy as it flies
Lives in Eternity's sun rise.

William Blake   *Notebook* (c. 1793)

THANKSGIVING FOR A NATIONAL VICTORY

HOWE'S OFF USHANT

Ye hypocrites, are these your pranks?
To murder men and give God thanks . . .

Robert Burns   c. 1794 Hogg and Motherwell, *Works* (1834–6)

Appearance may deceive thee – understand
A pure white glove may hide a filthy hand.

Anon   *London Magazine* 1824
From the German

Triumphant Demons stand, and Angels start,
To see the abysses of the human heart.

Walter Savage Landor   *Dry Sticks* (1858)

MEDITATIO

When I carefully consider the curious habits of dogs
I am compelled to conclude
That man is the superior animal.

When I consider the curious habits of man
I confess, my friend, I am puzzled.

Ezra Pound   *Lustra* (1916)

TO THE PREACHER

What's good alone is not enough to show,
But what's the good of good, we wish to know.

F. P. Barnard   *A Century of Epigram* (1916)
From the Latin of N. Catherinot

from NINETEEN HUNDRED AND NINETEEN

We, who seven years ago
Talked of honour and of truth,
Shriek with pleasure if we show
The weasel's twist, the weasel's tooth.

W. B. Yeats   *The Tower* (1928)

RETORT TO WHITMAN

And whoever walks a mile full of false sympathy
walks to the funeral of the whole human race.

D. H. Lawrence   *Last Poems* (1932)

RETORT TO JESUS

And whoever forces himself to love anybody
begets a murderer in his own body.

D. H. Lawrence   *Last Poems* (1932)

To stand up straight and tread the turning mill,
To lie flat and know nothing and be still,
Are the two trades of men; and which is worse
I know not, but I know that both are ill.

A. E. Housman   *More Poems* (1936)

Strange that a trick of light and shade could look
So like a living form that, first, I gave
The shadow mind and meaning : then, mistook
His will for mine; and, last, became his slave.

C. S. Lewis   *Poems* (1964)

Because he hates to praise by name
He praises everybody, Vice
And virtue must work much the same
To one who calls the whole world 'nice'.

James Michie *Martial : The Epigrams* (1978)

We've covered ground since that awkward day
When, thoughtlessly, a human mind
Decided to leave the apes behind,
Come pretty far, but who dare say
If far be forward or astray,
Or what we still might do in the way
Of patient building, impatient crime
Given the sunlight, salt and time.

W. H. Auden *About the House* (1966)

PHILOSOPHICAL

THE WORLD'S WHIRLIGIG

Plenty breeds Pride; Pride, Envy, Envy, War,
War, Poverty, Poverty humble Care.
Humility breeds Peace, and Peace breeds Plenty;
Thus round this World doth roll alternately.

Robert Hayman   *Quodlibets* (1628)

BUT MEN LOVED DARKNESS
RATHER THAN LIGHT

The worlds light shines, shine as it will,
The world will love its Darkness still:
I doubt though when the World's in Hell,
It will not love its Darkness half so well.

Richard Crashaw   *Steps to the Temple* (1646)

WORDS ARE WIND

Words are but wind that do from men proceed,
None but Chamelions on bare Air can feed:
Great men large hopeful promises may utter;
But words did never Fish or Parsnips butter.

John Taylor   *Epigrammes* (1651)

WORLDLY WEALTH

Wealth unto every man, I see,
Is like the bark unto the tree:
Take from the tree the bark away,
The naked tree will soon decay.
Lord, make me not too rich, nor make me poor.
To wait at rich men's tables, or their door.

Rowland Watkyns *Flamma Sine Fumo* (1662)

ON EPICURUS'S ATOMS

Observing the last Winter's show'rs of snow,
How thick the Flakes, and numberless did flow,
Crossing each other, hitting, often join'd,
It brought the Dance of Atoms to my Mind,
And narrowly I look'd upon the Ground,
To see what Figures they did there compound,
But arrant shapeless Snow was all I found:
Nor, I believe, on Salisbury's wide Plain,
(Unless by Rigour of the Cold was slain)
The Shepherds saw no Semblance of a Sheep,
Or the least Insect on the Earth does creep.
And much I fear, the Atomists wild Scheme
Of the World's Frame, is but a drowsy Dream:
The Plants, the Beasts, the Men, the Stars, the Sun
By interfering Particles begun,
Are only Maggots in their Brains that run.

Henry Killigrew *A Book of New Epigrams* (1695)

In bed we laugh, in bed we cry,
And born in bed, in bed we die;
The near approach a bed may show
Of human bliss to human woe.

Samuel Johnson   *Mrs Piozzi's Anecdotes* (1756)
From the French of Benserade

Beauty, without a Grace, may please the sight,
But ne'er can yield a permanent delight:
Thus round the hookless bait the pike will play;
Divert himself – but swim unhurt away.

Richard Graves   *Euphrosyne* (1780)
From the Greek of Nikarchus

The Worldly Hope men set their Hearts upon
Turns Ashes – or it prospers; and anon,
  Like Snow upon the Desert's dusty Face,
Lighting a little Hour or two – is gone.

Edward FitzGerald   *Rubáiyát of Omar Khayyám* 1st edn (1859)

A MEDITATION IN TIME OF WAR

For one throb of the artery,
While on that old grey stone I sat
Under the old wind-broken tree,
I knew that One is animate,
Mankind inanimate fantasy.

W. B. Yeats   *Michael Robartes and the Dancer* (1921)

mr youse needn't be so spry
concernin questions arty

each has his tastes but as for i
i likes a certain party

gimme the he-man's solid bliss
for youse ideas i'll match youse

a pretty girl who naked is
is worth a million statues

e. e. cummings   *is 5* (1926)

Whether determined by God or by their neural structure, still
All men have one common creed, account for it as you will:
The Truth is one and incapable of self-contradiction;
All knowledge that conflicts with itself is Poetic Fiction.

W. H. Auden   *Collected Shorter Poems 1930–44* (1950)

TO POSTERITY

When books have all seized up like the books in graveyards
And reading and even speaking have been replaced
By other, less difficult, media, we wonder if you
Will find in flowers and fruit the same colour and taste
They held for us for whom they were framed in words,
And will your grass be green, your sky be blue,
Or will your birds be always wingless birds?

Louis MacNeice   *Visitations* (1957)

ETERNITY AND THE CLOCK

A HOMAGE TO FINITY

Eternity's one of those mental blocks –
    the concept is inconceivable.
The clock concedes it in ticks and tocks,
    belittled, belaboured, believable.

Each passing moment is seized and chewed
    with argument incontestable
Premasticated, like baby food,
    eternity is digestable.

Piet Hein   *Still More Grooks* (1970)

ORIGIN

I went way back and asked the old
Ones deep in the graves, the youngest dead,
How language began, and who had the cred-
it of it, gods, men, devils, elves?
And this is the answer I was told:
'We got together one day,' they said,
'And talked it over among ourselves.'

Howard Nemerov   *The Western Approaches* (1975)

THE CONSOLATIONS OF NATURAL PHILOSOPHY

Always when there seems nothing left to do
there will be people, and the world, to view:
spectator pleasures and forget we know
the audience dies before the end of the show.

Alistair Elliot   *Contentions* (1977)

POLITICAL

Westminster is a mill which grinds all causes
And grind his cause for me then he that list:
For by demurs and pleas, appeals and clauses,
The toll is oft made greater than the grist.

Thomas Bastard   *Chrestoleros* (1598)

HEAVEN ON EARTH

Who make this earth their heaven whereon they dwell
Their heaven once past, must look to find an Hell.

John Heath   *Two Centuries of Epigrams* (1610)

IN VIRTUTEM★

Virtue we praise, but practice not her good,
(Athenian like) we act not what we know;
So many men do talk of Robin Hood,
Who never yet shot arrow in his bow.

Thomas Freeman   *Rubbe and a Great Cast* (1614)

★ On Virtue

The mouth speaks from the abundance of the heart,
So were we taught: but they have found an Art,
Lately at Westminster, which is far worse:
Most mouths speak from th'abundance of the purse.

John Heath   *The House of Correction* (1619)

ILL GOVERNMENT

Preposterous is that Government, (and rude)
When Kings obey the wilder Multitude.

Robert Herrick   *Hesperides* (1648)

MODERATION

In things a moderation keep,
Kings ought to shear, not skin their sheep.

Robert Herrick   *Hesperides* (1648)

UPON NERO'S QUINQUENNIUM

Till Sol had kiss'd the Equinoctial Line,
Ten times; in Nero, Virtues Rays did shine.
After five years, He did degenerate;
And prov'd a Vulture, to the Roman State.
Most Kings make Good beginnings; Few endure:
A Murtherer waits till He seems secure.

Thomas Pecke   *Parnassi Puerperium* (1659)

Earthquake is scarce acquainted with Scotch Ground:
Yet many Jolts of State have there been found.

Barten Holyday   *A Survey of the World* (1661)

UPON DEER FIGHTING

See how the tim'rous Herd in Fight engage!
How fearful Deer express the fiercest Rage!
Death from themselves they are not seen to fear!
Caesar, set on the Dogs, to save the Deer.

Henry Killigrew   *Epigrams of Martial, Englished* (1695)
From the Latin of Martial

ON THE DEATH OF THE QUEEN (MARY)

While our great Queen went bravely to the devil,
Our hero King was taken with the snivel.
Sure Death's a Jacobite that thus bewitches
Him to wear petticoats, and her the breeches.
We were mistaken in the choice our commanders;
Will should have knotted, and Moll have gone for Flanders.

Anon   *British Museum, M S Stowe 305* (1696)

UPON THE VOTE THAT PASS'D THAT THE CHURCH WAS NOT IN DANGER

When Anna was the Church's Daughter
She acted as her Mother taught her;
But now she's Mother of the Church,
She's left her Daughter in the Lurch.

Anon   *Poems on Affairs of State* (1707)

THE ODIOUS COMPARISON

A Whig, a Nettle, and a Toad,
Are much alike, by all that's Good:
The Nettle stings, the Whig he bites
The Swelling Toad his Venom spits:
But crush 'em all, your Strength exert,
And neither then can do you hurt.

Edward Ward(?)   *The Poetical Entertainer No 5* (1713)

THE BALANCE OF EUROPE

Now Europe's balanc'd, neither Side prevails
For nothing's left in either of the Scales.

Alexander Pope   *Miscellanies* (1727–28)

Whence this strange Bustle, Friends, I trow,
Of Tory, Whig; of High and Low?
  Zeal for the Public Good, no Doubt:
No; here's the Cause of all this Din;
They out of Place, wou'd fain come in,
  They that are in, wou'd not go out.

Hildebrand Jacob   *Works* (1733)

ON SEEING MISS AMBROSE, WITH AN ORANGE RIBBAND IN HER BREAST ON KING WILLIAM'S BIRTHDAY

Thou little Tory, where's the Jest,
 Of wearing Orange on thy Breast;
When that same Breast, insulting, shews
 The Whiteness of the Rebel Rose.

> Anon   *The Shamrock* Dublin (1742)

Whig and Tory scratch and bite,
 Just as hungry dogs we see:
Toss a bone 'twixt two, they fight,
 Throw a couple, they agree.

> Aaron Hill   *Works* (1753)

ON THE LATE INCREASE OF THE IRISH PEERAGE AND PENSION LIST

Irene wonders how the ruling pow'rs
Give Peers and Pensions in perpetual show'rs;
They search the Senates and explore the stews
For Pimps, Apostates, Infidels and Jews!

> Anon   *A Collection of Poems, Epigrams etc.*
> *Extracted from Newspapers* 1770–1795?

ON THE PRESENT WAR

A glorious war, John Bull, where the whole gain
Is *grinning honour*, for the thousands slain.
'T'is false say our allies, for John shall set
'Full fifty millions sterling – more in debt.'

Tom Paine(?)   *Tom Paine's Jests* (1794)

When Sampson full of wrath devis'd,
    Vengeance on false Philistia's race;
Three hundred foxes scarce suffer'd,
    To blaze destruction round the place.

'Three hundred,' says his grace, and smiles,
    'Alas! in my administration
'One single fox alone has wiles,
    'Sufficient to destroy a nation'.

Anon   *A Select Collection of Epigrams* (1796)

ON THE PARIS LOAN, CALLED
'THE LOAN UPON ENGLAND.'

The Paris cits, a patriotic band,
Advance their cash on British freehold land:
But let the speculating rogues beware –
They've bought the skin, but who's to kill the bear?

Anon   *The Anti Jacobin No. VIII* (1 January 1798)

THE SIMILE OF
ISAAC HAWKINS BROWNE, ESQ. M.P.

Of Augustus and Rome the poets still warble,
That he found it of brick, and he left it of marble:
So of Pitt and of England, they say, without vapour,
That he found it of gold, and he left it of paper.

Anon   *Morning Chronicle* (1806)

ENCLOSURES

The fault is great in man or woman
Who steals a goose from off a common;
But what can plead that man's excuse
Who steals a common from a goose?

Anon   *The Tickler Magazine* (1 February 1821)

REASON FOR THE CHOICE
OF A FOREIGN AMBASSADOR

Nature made Durham, I've strong suspicion,
With all this wormwood in his composition;
Like Hodgson's bitter ale, whose destination
Is not for home consumpt', but exportation.

Anon   *Blackwood's Magazine* (1838)

What is a communist? One who hath yearnings
For equal divisions of unequal earnings:
Idler, or bungler, or both, he is willing
To fork out his penny, and pocket your shilling.

> Ebenezer Elliot   *More Verse and Prose* (1850)

My Luds and Gents, who live at ease!
Since meek Bengal is far away,
Starve green-soul'd Hindoos, if you please,
By millions every year:
But don't starve yankee Canada!
And Ireland is too near.

> Ebenezer Elliot   *More Verse and Prose* (1850)

THE GEORGES

George the First was always reckoned
Vile, but viler George the Second;
And what mortal ever heard
Any good of George the Third?
When from earth the Fourth descended
(God be praised!) the Georges ended.

> Walter Savage Landor   *The Atlas* (28 April 1855)

BLACK AND WHITE

The Tories vow the Whigs are black as night,
And boast that they are only bless'd with light.
Peel's politics to both sides so incline,
He may be called the equinoctial line.

Anon   *The Jest Book* (1864)

ACCOUNTING FOR THE
APOSTACY OF MINISTERS

The Whigs, because they rat and change
    To Toryism, all must spurn;
Yet in the fact there's nothing strange
    That Wigs should twist, or curl, or turn.

Anon   *The Jest Book* (1864)

ON A BASE AGITATOR

A raw potato with a mouldy skin
Tossed on Irish harp, might boast of din.

Anon   *Political Epigrams 1874–1881*

ON BURKE

Oft have I heard that ne'er on Irish ground
A poisonous reptile ever yet was found;
Nature, though slow, will yet complete her work,
She saved her venom to create a Burke.

Warren Hastings   *Notes and Queries* (12 April 1851)

THE RT HON. B. DISRAELI, ON
BECOMING A PRIME MINISTER, 1874

And what is this small isle, after all,
Compared with the plains of Bengal,
Where millions are teeming,
Without ever dreaming
Of franchise or Exeter Hall?
John Bull shall look over the wall.

Anon   *Political Epigrams 1874–81*

A SUGGESTION MADE BY THE
POSTERS OF THE 'GLOBE'

The Globe, a paper of the Tories
(See the big posters stuck up here),
Depicts the name in which it glories,
And maps the southern hemisphere.

And oddly, too, it takes the pains
  To symbolise its readers' worth,
For that same hemisphere contains
  The lowest savages on earth.

J. E. Thorold Rogers   *Epistles, Satires, and Epigrams* (1876)

FREE EDUCATION

While Midas tears his hair that he
Should pay for Hodge's A B C,
His heart is torn with fears
That Hodge may learn to see his ears.

Anon   *The Epigram Club Collection* (1891)

TO A CERTAIN POLITICIAN

Let scanty soil upon your corpse be thrown,
That dogs may worry at it bone by bone.

F. P. Barnard   *A Century of Epigrams* (1916)

EPITAPH ON A POLITICIAN

Here richly, with ridiculous display,
The Politician's corpse was laid away.
While all of his acquaintance sneered and slanged
I wept: for I had longed to see him hanged.

Hilaire Belloc   *Sonnets and Verse* (1923)
After the French of Malherbe

LORD ROTHERMERE

Faith – culture – statecraft : which of these avails
Against the rising tide of Record Sales?
'Tis we, the People, rule, and ruling, seek
The less elusive cult of Pip and Squeak.

Hubert Phillips   *A Diet of Crisps* (1929)

THE GREAT DAY

Hurrah for revolution and more cannon-shot!
A beggar upon horseback lashes a beggar on foot.
Hurrah for revolution and cannon come again!
The beggars have changed places, but the lash goes on.

W. B. Yeats   *Last Poems* (1939)

TO NEARLY EVERYONE IN EUROPE TODAY

A war to save civilisation, you say?
Then what have *you* to do with it, pray?
Some attempt to acquire it would show truer love
Than fighting for something you know nothing of.

Hugh MacDiarmid   written c. 1940 *Collected Poems* (1967)

EPITAPH ON A TYRANT

Perfection, of a kind, was what he was after,
And the poetry he invented was easy to understand;
He knew human folly like the back of his hand,
And was greatly interested in armies and fleets;
When he laughed, respectable senators burst with laughter
And when he cried the little children died on the streets.

W. H. Auden *Another Time* (1940)

FASCIST SPEAKER

Armoured like a rhinoceros
He hurls his tons into the crowd
From half a dozen minds he rips
Triangles of flesh and blood.

Six shouts, six cardboard banners rise
Daubed with slogans saying Pain
But wilt and tear in the hundredfold
Applause of men as mild as rain.

Adrian Mitchell *Poems* (1964)

REMEMBER SUEZ?

England, unlike junior nations
Wears officers' long combinations
So no embarrassment was felt
By the Church, the Government or the Crown.
But I saw the Thames like a grubby old belt
And England's trousers falling down.

Adrian Mitchell   *Poems* (1964)

OVID IN THE THIRD REICH

NON PECCAT, QUAECUMQUE POTEST PECCASSE NEGARE,
SOLAQUE FAMOSAM CULPA PROFESSA FACIT.
(AMORES, III, XIV)

I love my work and my children. God
Is distant, difficult. Things happen.
Too near the ancient troughs of blood
Innocence is no earthly weapon.

I have learned one thing: not to look down
So much upon the damned. They, in their sphere,
Harmonise strangely with the divine
Love. I, in mine, celebrate the love-choir.

Geoffrey Hill   *King Log* (1968)

UPON THE KING'S RETURN FROM FLANDERS

Rejoice you sots, your idol's come again,
To pick your pockets and kidnap your men.
Give him your moneys, and his Dutch your lands.
Ring not your bells ye fools, but wring your hands.

Henry Hall   *B.S. M.S. Stove 305* (1696)

PROSPECTING THE SUMMIT

A GROOK ABOUT PARLOUR GAMES

Those who've been making the week go by
trying to work out exactly whom, with
what reservations, and how, and why,
who would (or wouldn't) remain in the room with,

Or to consider, anent their doom,
a further point they can play the goat with,
viz : to discover exactly whom
who might (or mightn't) be in the same boat with.

Piet Hein   *Still More Grooks* (1970)

POWER TO THE PEOPLE

Why are the stamps adorned with kings and presidents?
That we may lick their hinder parts and thump their heads.

Howard Nemerov   *Gnomes & Occasions* (1973)

THE AMBIGUOUS FATE OF GIEVE PATEL, HE BEING NEITHER MUSLIM NOR HINDU IN INDIA

To be no part of this hate is deprivation.
Never could I claim a circumsized butcher
Mangled a child out of my arms, never rave
At the milk-bibing, grass-guzzling hypocrite
Who pulled off my mother's voluminous
Robes and sliced away at her dugs.
Planets focus their fires
Into a worm of destruction
Edging along the continent. Bodies
Turn ashen and shrivel. I
Only burn my tail.

Gieve Patel   *How Do You Withstand, Body* (1976)

NO TROUBLE

Socialism, like the Sermon on the Mount,
The Tories say is much too difficult for men. So then?
Since Toryism, torture, hatred, greed, come
Easily to men, let's plump for them.

Geoffrey Grigson   *The Cornish Dancer* (1982)

A GRAIN OF SALT

Swords into ploughshares, what a simple thing
Isaiah wished for, when compared to this
Stunning free offer from a pair of king-
doms come to trade their nukes in on a kiss

And chicken on the world's great suicide pact,
Agreed by treaty that on the deciding day
Conjoined in one big hard-to-follow act
Both tribes will throw their boomerangs away.

Howard Nemerov   *Inside the Onion* (1984)

SARTORIAL

OF CODRUS

Into a princely Palace proud
   (built brave with Marble stone)
With ragged tattered torn attire
   poor Codrus would have gone.

So nakt (quoth one) ye come not here:
   quoth Codrus no, and why?
The gods are nakt, and none but nakt
   must go to heaven perdie.

    Timothe Kendall   *Flowres of Epigrammes* (1577)
    From the Latin of Simon Vallambertus Avalon

DE ADAM PRIMO HOMINE*

When Adam covered his first nakedness
With fig tree leaves he did, he knew not what.
The leaves were good indeed, but not for that,
God ordain'd skins 'gainst his skin's wretchedness.
But 'gainst diseases and our inward need,
To piece our life which flitting still doth pass.
What leaf do we not use, what herb, what grass,
Their secret virtues standing us in stead?
    Thus in our garments these we cast away:
    And yet our life doth wear them everyday.

Thomas Bastard   *Chrestoleros* (1598)

AGAINST GAUDY-BRAGGING-UNDOUGHTY DACCUS

Daccus is all bedaub'd with golden lace,
   Hose, doublet, jerkins, and gamashes too;
Yet is he foolish, rude and beastly-base;
Crows like a cock, but like a craven does:
   Then he's (to prise him nought his worth beneath)
   A leaden rapier in a golden sheath.

John Davies of Hereford   *The Scourge of Folly* (1611)

* On Adam, the first man.

Sir, can you tell where young Pandorus lives,
That was surnamed here the *prodigal*:
He that so much for his silk stockings gives
Till nought is left to buy him shoes withal?
    Oh blame him not, to make what shew he can,
    How should he else be thought a Gentleman.

Henry Parrot   *Laquei Ridiculosi* (1613)

ON ENGLISH MONSIEUR

Would you believe, when you this monsieur see,
    That his whole body should speak French, not he?
That so much scarf of France, and hat, and feather,
    And shoe, and tie, and garter should come hither
And land on one whose face durst never be
    Toward the sea, farther than half-way tree?
That he, untravelled, should be French so much,
    As Frenchmen in his company should seem Dutch?
Or had his father, when he did him get,
    The French disease, with which he labours yet?
Or hung some monsieur's picture on the wall,
    By which his dam conceived him, clothes and all?
Or is it some French statue? No: it doth move,
    And stoop, and cringe. Oh, then it needs must prove
The new French tailor's motion, monthly made,
    Daily to turn in Paul's and help the trade.

Ben Jonson   *Workes* (1616)

DON FASHIONISTA

French, Spanish, Dutch, Italian, Indian Ape,
A mighty linguist if his Clothes could speak,
A man, (yet of a most inhuman shape)
And wonder not if he his promise break
For he that hath engag'd unto so many
His little Faith, hath left himself not any.

Joseph Martyn   *New Epigrams* (1621)

AN EPIGRAM ON AN OLD UNHANDSOME, YET LUSTFULL WOMAN: WHO WAS DISCOVERED TO WEAR DRAWERS OF BLACK TAFFETA

The devil's in't : did ever Witch
In mourning cloth her wrinkled breech?
Unless the Incubus were dead
That had her wither'd maidenhead?
Why that part veil'd? the face left free,
That hath no less deformity?
A pox on both, the reason's smelt:
She'd have one seen, the other felt
    That neither sense into mislike may grow,
    Though she be light, she keeps all dark below.

Thomas Nabbes
Plays, Masks, Epigrams, Elegies and Epithalamiums (1639)

DELIGHT IN DISORDER

A sweet disorder in the dress
Kindles in clothes a wantonness:
A Lawn about the shoulders thrown
Into a fine distraction:
An erring Lace, which here and there
Enthralls the Crimson Stomacher:
A Cuff neglectful, and thereby
Ribbands to flow confusedly:
A winning wave (deserving Note)
In the tempestuous petticoat:
A careless shoe-string, in whose tie
I see a wild civility:
Do more bewitch me, than when Art
Is too precise in every part.

Robert Herrick   *Hesperides* (1648)

LEARNING AND DRESS

Adorn not more your body than your brains;
Lest that this emblem in your teeth be flung,
That you resemble houses, which remain
With empty garrets though the rooms be hung.

Henry Delaune   *ΠΑΤΡΙΚΟΝ ΔΩRON* (1651)

A GREAT WITCH

Pride is a Witch, few from her charms escape,
She turns us daily into sundry shapes:
She hath her spirits, who do work like Thrashers
Mercers, soft Silk-men, Tailors, Haberdashers.

John Taylor   *Epigrammes* (1651)

In dismal Weeds you still appear,
    Melissa, tho' the Time is out,
And vow, your Mourning ne'er shall end:
    Excess of Grief, I make no Doubt,
For our departed, loving Friend;
Yet, since you have not shed a Tear,
    There are some People who pretend,
It can't be *sorrow* for your Dear.
    'Tis true, this Dress becomes you more,
    Than any Thing you ever wore.

Hildebrand Jacob   *Works* (1735)

ON THE LADIES HOOPS AND
HATS NOW WORN

Our Granums of Old were so piously nice,
That to shew us their shoe-tie was reckon'd a Vice:
But, Lord! could they now but peep out of the Ground,
And see the fine Fashions their Daughters have found;
How their Steps they reveal, and oblige the lewd Eye
With the Legs pretty Turn and delicate Thigh:
Which the Modern Free Hoops, so ample and wide,
Up-lift the fair smocks with an impudent Pride.
And betray the sweet graces they chastly should hide.
But how wanton is Beauty? how capricious the Fair?
Their Hats are all flapp'd with so modest an Air;
Each Virgin you meet, a veil'd Vestal you'd swear.
In Propriety strange! How wild the Extremes!
How the Hats suit the Hoops! just like Water and Flames.
What Whimsies are these? What comical Farces?
They hide all their faces, and shew us their Ar—s.
But from hence an excuse for the Ladies may rise;
For when conscious their Nethermost charms treat our Eyes,
Perhaps they may blush; and 'tis a Sign of some grace,
When their Breech is expos'd, to cover their Face.

Anon   *British Museum 1872 a.1* (c. 1740)

ON THE LADIES WEARING LARGE HOOPS

The fam'd Lycurgus found a Way
    By Garments Rent, ('tis said)
The Female Beauties to display,
    To tempt the Youth to wed.

But had the prudent Spartan known,
  The Use of Hoops so wide;
Without those Arts, they might have shown
  What here no Women hide.

John Winstanley   *Poems* (1742)

LORD FOPPINGTON'S PROPOSAL
TO PARLIAMENT

He thinks, it might advance the Nation's Trade,
Were a law made, no Tailor shou'd be paid.

Anon   *Epigrams in Distich* (1748)

Did ladies now (as we are told
Our great-grandmother did of old)
Wake to a sense of blasted fame,
The fig-tree spoil to hide their shame,
So num'rous are those modern Eves,
A Forest scarce could find them leaves.

Anon   *The Festival of Love* (c. 1770)

Each Bond-street buck conceits, unhappy elf!
He shews his *clothes*! Alas! he shews himself.
O that they knew, these overdrest self-lovers,
What hides the body oft the mind discovers.

Samuel Taylor Coleridge   *Morning Post* (11 October 1802)

IMPROMPTU

UPON BEING OBLIGED TO LEAVE A PLEASANT PARTY, FROM THE WANT OF A PAIR OF BREECHES TO DRESS FOR DINNER IN

Between Adam and me the great difference is,
  Though a paradise each has been forc'd to resign,
That he never wore breeches, till turn'd out of his,
  While for want of my breeches, I'm banished from mine.

Thomas Moore   Written 1810 *Poetical Works* (1841)

NUDITY AT THE CAPITAL

But nakedness, woolen massa, concerns an innermost atom.
If that remains concealed, what does the bottom matter?

Wallace Stevens   *Ideas of Order* (1935)

Yours is a classic dilemma, Lesbia;
whenever you get up from your chair
your clothes treat you most indecently.
Tugging and talking, with right hand and left
you try to free the yards of cloth swept
up your fundament. Tears and groans
are raised to Heaven as the imperilled
threads are pulled to safety from
those deadly straits: the huge Symplegades
of your buttocks grip all that pass.
What should you do to avoid such
terrible embarrassment? Ask Uncle Val –
don't get up girl, and don't sit down!

Peter Porter   *After Martial* (1973)
After the Latin of Martial

SATIRICAL

PLOCHE, OR THE DOUBLER

Yet when I saw my self to you was true,
I loved my self, because my self loved you.

Sir Walter Scott   Puttenham, *The Arte of English Poesie* (1589)

IN SEUERUM*

The puritan Severus oft doth read,
This text that doth pronounce vain speech a sin,
That thing defiles a man that doth proceed
From out the mouth, not that which enters in.
Hence is it, that we seldom hear him swear,
And thereof like a Pharisee he vaunts,
But he devours more Capons in a year,
Than would suffice a hundred protestants.
And sooth those sectaries are gluttons all,
As well the thread-bare Cobbler as the Knight,
For those poor slaves which have not wherewithal
Feed on the rich, till they devour them quite.
　　And so like Pharoes kine, the eat up clean
　　Those that be fat, yet still themselves be lean.

Sir John Davies   *Epigrammes and Elegies* (159–?)

* On Severus

IN CAUIM*

Caius hath brought from foreign lands
A sooty wench with many hands.
Which do in golden letters say
She is his wife not stolen away.
He might have sav'd with small discretion
Paper, ink, and all confession.
   For none that seeth her face and making,
   Will judge her stol'n but by mistaking.

Thomas Bastard   *Chrestoleros* (1598)

Severus is extreme in eloquence,
In perfum'd words, plung'd over head and ears,
He doth create rare Phrase, but rarer sense,
Fragments of Latin, all about he bears.
Unto his servingman, alias, his boy,
He utters speech exceeding quaint and coy.

Deminutive, and my defective slave,
Reach my corps coverture immediately:
My pleasures pleasure is, the same to have,
T'ensconce my person from frigidity.
His man believes all's Welsh, his Master spoke,
Till he rails English: Rouge, go fetch my Cloak.

Samuel Rowlands
The Letting of Humours Blood in the Head Vaine (1600)

* On Caius

128

Kate can fancy only beardless husbands,
That's the cause she shakes off ev'ry suiter,
That's the cause she lives to stale a virgin,
For before her heart can heat her answer,
Her smooth youth she finds all hugely bearded.

Thomas Campion
Observations in the Art of English Poesie (1602)

Lieutenant Lentelus lives discontent,
    and much repineth at the want of wars:
For when his credit, coin, all is spent,
    What should he do, but idly curse the stars.
Content thee Lentelus with thine estate,
That wert not idle when thou stolest the plate.

Henry Parrot   *The Mous-Trap* (1606)

IN FLORIDAM*

I offered Florida a Kiss, and she,
Diffring from use, turn'd her left cheek to me,
Some who stood by, did much commend her fort,
Because it was a fashion used in court.
    I take't her kindness rather, cause I think,
    She turned her cheek, because her mouth did stink.

Richard West   *Wit's ABC* (1608)

* On Florida

A COVERTITE

Strangely addicted now is Brutus found,
He doth suppose the world is at an end:
He will not drink nor ramble foot of ground,
Nor take a pipe neither with foe or friend.
He meditates on heaven, no, 'tis not so,
Another place he thinks on which is low:
O 'tis his purse which nere doth measure keep,
He cannot reach a penny 'tis so deep.

Roger Sharpe   *More Fooles Yet* (1610)

TOM TELLS TROTH

My love sayth Tristram is as constant sure,
As is the Moon, Diana, chaste and pure:
Credit his words, assured true they be,
The Moon doth change each month, and so doth she.

Roger Sharpe   *More Fooles Yet* (1610)

IN PORCUM★

Porcus that foul unsociable hog,
Grunts me out this still: *Love me, love my dog.*
And reason is there why we should so do,
Since that his dog's the lovelier of the two.

John Heath   *Two Centuries of Epigrams* (1610)

★ On Porcus

AGAINST BATTUS THAT BUYS BOOKS
TO STAY HIS STUDIES STOMACH

Battus doth brag he hath a world of books,
His studie's maw holds more than well it may;
But seld or never he upon them looks;
And yet he looks upon them everyday:
He looks upon their out-side, but within
He never looks, nor ever will begin;
   Because it clean against his nature goes
To know mens secrets; so, he keeps them close.

John Davies of Hereford   *The Scourge of Folly* (1611)

Caecus awak't, was told the sun appear'd
Which had the darkness of the morning clear'd:
But Caecus sluggish thereto makes reply;
The Sun hath further far to go than I.

Henry Parrot   *The Mastive* (1615)

ON BANCK THE USURER

Banck feels no lameness of his knotty gout;
   His moneys travel for him, in and out;
And though the soundest legs go every day,
   He toils to be at hell, as soon as they.

Ben Jonson   *Workes* (1616)

ON SPIES

Spies, you are lights in state, but of base stuff,
Who, when you've burnt yourselves down to the snuff,
Stink, and are thrown away. End fair enough.

Ben Jonson   *Workes* (1616)

UPON MILO

Milo believes and hath a wager laid,
The world will end within these fourteen years,
By whom or where the money shall be paid,
But if he wins is Milo's only fear.

Henry Peacham   *Thalia's Baquet* (1620)

KLOCKIUS

Klockius so deeply hath sworn, n'er more to come
In baudy house, that he dares not go home.

John Donne   *Poems* (1633)

PHRYNE

Thy flattering picture, Phryne, is like thee,
Only in this, that you both painted be.

John Donne   *Poems* (1633)

ON A POT-POET

What lofty verses Caelus writes? it is,
But when his head with wine oppressed is,
So when great drops of rain fall from the skies
In standing pools, huge bubbles will arise.

Anon   Witt's Recreations (1640)

TWO WENT UP INTO THE TEMPLE TO PRAY

Two went to pray? O rather say
One went to brag, th'other to pray:
One stands up close and treads on high,
Where th'other dares not send his eye.
One nearer to God's Altar trod,
The other to the Altar's God.

Richard Crashaw   Steps to the Temple (1646)

UPON GREEDY

An old, old widow Greedy needs wo'd wed,
Not for affection to her, or her Bed;
But in regard, 'twas often said, this old
Woman wo'd bring him more than co'd be told,
He took her; now the jest in this appears,
So old she was, that none co'd tell her years.

Robert Herrick   Hesperides (1648)

CONCERNING SUCH AS OF LATE HAVE RECEIVED THE HONOUR, SOME OF LORD, SOME OF EARL, BY THE NAME OF EMINENT RUNNING WATERS

I know no reason why, in Scotland, divers
    Have built their dignities upon the brittle
Unstay'd foundation of impetuous rivers,
    None fearing, that therein he sink his title;
    Unless it be, they aim by such a wile,
    T'have without eloquence a fluent style.

Anon   *Ex Ungue Leonem* (1654)

As I remember, Aelia cought full sore
She cought out twice two Teeth, she had but four.
Now she may safely cough for ever – why?
Her mouth's not charg'd to let such Bullets fly.

Charles Cotton   *Poems on Several Occasions* (1689)
From the Latin of Martial

ON LESBIA

Lesbia talks Bawdy, and does Water drink,
Thou dost well, Lesbia, so to wash the Sink.

Henry Killigrew   *Epigrammes of Martial, Englished* (1695)
From the Latin of Martial

A FOUNTAIN OF A TRITON, AT THE
PALACE OF BARBERINI

What makes thy Rover hither come,
Why rambles he so far from home?
Doth he dislike the Sea d'ye think,
And comes fresh Water here to drink;
Or of some Nymph has made a Strumpet,
And now retires to save his Trumpet;
Or Rocks and Monsters comes t'avoid,
For fear of being soon destroy'd?
O Triton, think not here t'evade all shocks,
Rome has its Monsters too and *dang'rous Rocks*.

John Elsum
*Epigrams upon the Paintings of
the Most Eminent Masters* (1700)

LESBIA

When Lesbia first I saw so heavenly fair,
With eyes so bright, and with that awful air,
I thought my heart, which durst so high aspire,
As bold as his who snatch'd celestial fire.
But soon as e'er the beauteous idiot spoke,
Forth from her coral lips such folly broke,
Like balm the trickling nonsense heal'd my wound,
And what her eyes enthrall'd her tongue unbound.

William Congreve   Dryden, *Miscellany* V (1704)

Whilst in the dark on thy soft hand I hung
And heard the tempting siren in thy tongue
What flames, what darts, what anguish I endur'd!
But when the candle enter'd I was cur'd.

Richard Steele   *Spectator No 52* (30 April 1711)
From the Latin of Martial

(ON CATO'S ENTRY INTO THE ROMAN THEATRE, WHEN THE FLORALIA WERE TO BE PERFORMED)

Why dost thou come, great Censor of the age,
To see the loose diversions of the stage?
With awful countenance, and brow severe.
What in the name of goodness dost thou here?
See the mixt crowd! how giddy, lewd and vain!
Didst thou come in but to go out again?

Joseph Addison   *Spectator No 446* (1 August 1712)
From the Latin of Martial

Thy Nags (the leanest Things alive)
So very hard Thou lov'st to drive;
I heard, thy anxious Coach-man say,
It costs Thee more in Whips, than Hay.

Matthew Prior   *Poems on Several Occasions* (1718)

A TRUE MAID

No, no; for my Virginity,
    When I lose that, says Rose, I'll die:
Behind the Elms, last Night, cry'd Dick,
    Rose, were You not extremely Sick?

       Matthew Prior   *Poems on Several Occasions* (1718)

You beat your Pate, and fancy Wit will come:
    Knock as you please, there's no body at home.

       Alexander Pope   *Miscellanies* (1732)

PROPER INGREDIENTS TO MAKE A SCEPTIC

Would you, my Friend, a finish'd Sceptic make,
To form his Nature, these Materials take:
A little Learning; twenty Grains of Sense,
Join'd with a double share of Ignorance;
Infuse a little Wit into the skull,
Which never fails to make a mighty Fool;
Two Drams of Faith; a Ton of Doubting next;
Let all be with the Dregs of Reason mixt:
When, in his Mind, these jarring seeds are sown,
He'll censure all Things, but approve of none.

       Stephen Duck   *Poems on Several Occasions* (1736)

TO THE ROYAL SOCIETY

If the perpetual motion you would know;
The Thames, and Tattle's tongue, for ever flow.

Anon   *Epigrams in Distich* (1740)

EPIGRAM ON A CERTAIN EFFIMINATE PEER

As Nature H—'s Clay was blending,
Uncertain what the Work could end in,
Whether a Female or a Male,
A Pin dropt in and turn'd the Scale.

John Winstanley   *Poems* (1742)

TO THE GALLICAN KING

To finish your wars, as you want fresh supplies,
    Where next shall your marshals for succour repair?
In the clouds they have always good trusty allies,
    For the devils they tell us inhabit the air.

Thomas Newcomb   *Novus Epigrammation Delectus* (1760)

ON A PALE LADY

Whence comes it that, in Clara's face
The Lily only has a place? –
Is it, that the absent rose
Is gone to paint her husband's nose?

Anon   *The Christmas Treat* (1767)

A cushion, for the soft place meet
Our grandams bottoms us'd to greet;
From moderns that old fashion's fled,
Their softest place is on the head.

Anon   *A Collection of Poems, Epigrams, etc.*
Extracted From Newspapers (1770–95?)

ON A BAD SINGER

When screech-owls scream, their note portends
To frightened mortals death of friends:
But when Corvino strains his throat,
Even screech-owls sicken at the note.

Richard Graves   *Euphrosyne* (1780)
From the Greek of Lucilius

EPIGRAM ON MR QUIN'S SAYING THAT 'GARRICK WAS A NEW RELIGION,' AND THAT 'WHITEFIELD WAS FOLLOWED FOR A TIME, BUT THEY WOULD ALL COME TO CHURCH AGAIN'.

Pope Quin, who damns all churches but his own,
Complains that heresy corrupts the town:
'That Whitefield Garrick has misled the age,
'And taints the sound religion of the stage;
'Schism, he cries, has turn'd the nation's brain;
'But eyes will open, and to church again!'
Thou great infallible, for fear to roar,
Thy bulls and errors are rever'd no more;
When doctrines meet with gen'ral approbation,
It is not heresy, but reformation.

David Garrick   *Poetical Works* (1785)

Her whole life is an Epigram smart, smooth & neatly pen'd
Platted quite neat to catch applause with a sliding noose at
the end.

William Blake   *Notebook* (c. 1793)

When I called t'other day on a noble renowned,
In his great marble hall lay the Bible, well bound;
Nor printed by Basket, and bound up in black,
But chained to the floor, like a thief, by the back.
Unacquainted with tone, and your quality airs,
I supposed it intended for family prayers.
His piety pleased, I applauded his zeal,
Yet thought none would venture the Bible to steal;
But judge my surprise when informed of the case, –
He had chained it for fear it would fly in his face!

Anon   *Cumberland Journal* (27 October 1798)

When I see a Rubens, Rembrandt, Correggio
I think of the Crippled Harry & Slobbering Joe
And then I question thus: are artists rules
To be drawn from the works of two manifest fools?
Then God defend us from the Arts I say.
Send Battle, Murder, Sudden death, O pray.
Rather than be such a blind Human Fool
I'd be an Ass, a Hog, a worm, a Chair, a Stool.

William Blake   *Notebook* (1810–11)

From Virtue's path when Kitty strays,
A concious blush her guilt betrays;
No wonder then they err who say,
That Kitty paints both night and day.

William Barnes Rhodes *Epigrams* (1803)

While Fell was reposing himself on the hay,
A reptile conceal'd bit his leg as he lay;
But, all venom himself, of the wound he made light,
And got well, while the scorpion died of the bite.

J. & H. L. Hunt *Fables and Epigrams* (1825)
From the German of Lessing

FRITZ

Quoth gallant Fritz 'I ran away
To fight again another day.'
The meaning of his speech is plain,
He only fled to fly again.

J. & H. L. Hunt *Fables and Epigrams* (1825)
From the German of Lessing

A SPECULATION

Of all the speculations the market holds forth,
The best that I know for a lover of pelf,
Were to buy friend James up at the price he is worth,
And sell him at that which he sets himself!

Thomas Moore *Poetical Works* (1841)

A SENSIBLE GIRL'S REPLY TO MOORE'S 'OUR COUCH SHALL BE ROSES ALL SPANGLED WITH DEW'

It would give me rheumatics, and so it would you.

Walter Savage Landor   *Dry Sticks* (1858)

Such the protuberance that abuts
From pope's and king's enormous guts,
That to shake hands should either try,
A flock of geese between might fly,
And any parley would require
Some fathoms of electric wire.

Walter Savage Landor   *Heroic Idylls* (1863)

ON THE COLUMN TO THE DUKE OF YORK'S MEMORY

In former times the illustrious dead were burned,
Their hearts preserved in sepulchre inurned;
This column, then, commemorates the part
Which custom makes us single out – the heart;
You ask, 'How by a column this is done?'
I answer, *''Tis a hollow thing of stone.'*

Anon   *The Jest Book* (1864)

TEMPUS EDAX RERUM*

'Time is money,' Robin says;
   'Tis true; I'll prove it clear, –
Tom owes ten pounds, for which he pays
   In limbo, half a year.

                    Anon   *The Wild Garland* (1866)

THE BOSS

Skilled to pull wires, he baffles Nature's hope,
Who sure intended him to stretch a rope.

        James Russell Lowell   *Heartsease and Rue* (1888)

LORD FINCHLEY

Lord Finchley tried to mend the electric light
Himself. It struck him dead: And serve him right!
It is the business of the wealthy man
To give employment to the artisan.

              Hilaire Belloc   *More Peers* (1911)

* Time, the devourer of things.

ON LADY POLTAGRUE : A PUBLIC DEVIL

The Devil, having nothing else to do,
Went off to tempt my Lady Poltagrue.
My Lady, tempted by a private whim,
To his annoyance, tempted him.

Hilaire Belloc   *Sonnets and Verse* (1923)

This humanist whom no beliefs constrained
Grew so broadminded he was scatter-brained.

J. V. Cunningham   *The Judge is Fury* (1947)

A FINANCIER

He was too nice for common theft
Too sensitive for vulgar crime:
Less crude than other snails, he left
No trace of silver slime.

George Rostrevor Hamilton   *The Carved Stone* (1952)

Lady, a better sculptor far
Chiselled those curves you smudge and mar,

And God did more than lipstick can
To justify your mouth to man.

C. S. Lewis   *Poems* (1964)

Furious, your little villa feels the cold,
But there's no wind of the compass you can hold
Responsible for that. What makes you freeze
Is a cool fifteen thousand sesterces
Of mortgage. Horrible, pestilential breeze!

> James Michie   *The Poems of Catullus* (1972)
> From the Latin of Catullus

Hermogenes is rather short,
He looks up microbes mini-skirts,
And high above him, snowy-topped
Loom peaks of objects that he's dropped.

> Peter Porter   *The Greek Anthology* (1973)
> After the Greek of Lucilius

When you send out invitations, don't ask me.
Its rare filets that I like not filigree.
A piece of pumpkin each! The table creaks
not with the weight of food but your antiques.

Save your *soirées* for connoisseurs who'll notch
their belts in tighter for a chance to watch
the long procession of your silverware,
for art's sake happy just to stand and stare,
and, for some fine piece to goggle at, forgo
all hope of eating, if the hallmarks show.

> Tony Harrison   *Palladas : Poems* (1975)
> After the Greek of Palladas

CAPITALS

When a common noun becomes a Proper One
It seems to add an invisible *de* or *von*,
Gets uppity, forgets its former friends
And can't remember even what it means.

Look at intelligence. It went that way
As soon as ever it joined the CIA;
And the dozen gods themselves turned odd
The minute they got upped in grade to God.

Howard Nemerov   *The Western Approaches* (1975)

SCATOLOGICAL

OF BLOWING

What wind can there blow, that doth not some man please?
A fart in the blowing doth the blower ease.

John Heywood *An Hundred Epigrammes* (1550)

IN SALIUM

When Salius takes the pen in hand, he brags
He'll rouse his wit to raise the price of rags;
And writes such verses as stand men in stead
For Privy business rather than to read.
Now pray you when the paper lies besh—
How are rags raised by his rousing wit?

Thomas Freeman *Rubbe and a Great Cast* (1614)

A nice young Dame that long'd for dainty Cates,
    With her that sold them thus expostulates:
    My Nose (I hope) shall be my Cook (quoth she)
Mine Arse (quoth th'other) may your kitchen be.

Henry Parrot *The Mastive* (1615)

OF GARLIC, TO MY LADY ROGERS

If Leeks you like, and do the smell dislike,
Eat Onions, and you shall not smell the Leek:
If you of Onions would the scent expel,
Eat Garlic, that will drown th'onion's smell,
   But sure, gainst Garlic's favour, at one word,
   I know but one receipt, what's that? (Go look.)

Sir John Harington
The Most Elegant and Wittie Epigrams (1618)
From the Latin of Thomas More

UPON UMBER

Umber was painting of a Lion fierce,
And working it, by chance from Umber's Arse
Flew out a crack, so mighty, that the Fart,
(As Umber swears) did make his Lion start.

Robert Herrick   *Hesperides* (1648)

(EPITAPH ON THE FART IN THE PARLIAMENT HOUSE)

Reader, I was born and cried,
Crackt so, smelt so, and so died,
Like to Caesar's was my death,
He in senate lost his breath;
And alike interr'd doth lie,
Thy famous Romulus and I.
And at last, like Flora fair,
I left the Commonwealth mine air.

John Hoskyns   *Musarum Deliciae* (1655)

ON MANNEJA

That thy Dog loves to lick thy lips, th'art pleas'd:
He'll lick that too, of which thy Belly's eas'd;
And not to flatter, and the Truth to smother,
I do believe, he knows not one from t'other.

Henry Killigrew   *Epigrams of Martial, Englished* (1695)
From the Latin of Martial

Gustillo, with a witless Face,
Damns ev'ry Stroke that aims at Grace,
   But praises each mean Thought or Word.
Thus Flies, begot in stupid Stinks,
Leaving the Vi'lets, Roses, Pinks,
   Buzz round, and settle on a—.

James Drake
The Humours of New Tunbridge Wells at Islington (1734)

ON A F--T

My Age is not a Moment's Stay;
My Birth the same with my Decay:
I savour ill; no Colour know;
And fade, the Instant that I blow.

Jonathan Swift(?)   *The Nut Cracker* (1751)

SEPULCHRAL

EPITAPH : IOHANNIS SANDE

Who would live in others breath?
Fame deceives the dead man's trust.
Since our names are chang'd in death
Sand I was, and now am dust.

Thomas Bastard   *Chrestoleros* (1598)

ON A WHORE

One stone sufficeth (lo what death can do)
Her that in life was not content with two.

John Hoskyns   Camden, *Remaines* (1605)

IN BEATRICEM PRAEPROPERE DEFUNCTAM★

In Beatrice did all perfections grow,
That she could wish or nature could bestow.
When death enamor'd with that excellence
Straight grew in love with her, and took her hence.

John Heath   *Two Centuries of Epigrams* (1610)

★ On Beatrice Hastily Deceased.

(EPITAPH ON JOHN COMBE, AN USURER)

Ten in the hundred the devil allows,
But Combes will have twelve he swears and he vows:
If any one ask, who lies in this tomb,
Hoh! quoth the devil, 'tis my John O'Combe.

William Shakespeare
written 1614 Aubrey, *Brief Lives* (1669–1696)

ON MY FIRST SON

Farewell, thou child of my right hand, and joy;
   My sin was too much hope of thee, loved boy.
Seven years thou wert lent to me, and I thee pay,
   Exacted by thy fate, on the just day.
Oh, could I lose all father now! For why
   Will man lament the state he should envy?
To have so soon 'scaped world's and flesh's rage,
   And, if no other misery, yet age?
Rest in soft peace, and, asked, say here doth lie
   Ben Jonson his best piece of poetry;
For whose sake, henceforth, all his vows be such,
   As what he loves may never like too much.

Ben Jonson   *Workes* (1616)

THE AUTHOR'S EPITAPH, MADE BY HIMSELF

Even such is Time, which takes in trust
Our Youth, our Joys, and all we have,
And pays us but with age and dust,
Who in the dark and silent grave,
When we have wandered all our ways,
Shuts up the story of our days:
And from which Earth, and Grave, and Dust,
The Lord shall raise me up I trust.

Sir Walter Raleigh
The Prerogative of Parliaments In England (1628)

HERO AND LEANDER

Both rob'd of air, we both lie in one ground,
Both of whom one fire had burnt, one water drowned.

John Donne   *Poems* (1633)

EPITAPH ON BIBULUS

Here, who but once in's life did thirst, doth lie,
Perhaps the dust may make him once more dry.

Robert Heath   *Clarastella* (1650)

EPITAPH ON ANNE PRIDEAUX, DAUGHTER OF DR PRIDEAUX, REGIUS PROFESSOR, WHO DIED AT THE AGE OF SIX YEARS

Nature in this small volume was about
To perfect what in women was left out.
Yet fearful lest a piece so well begun
Might want preservatives when she had done,
Ere she could finish what she undertook
Threw dust upon it and shut up the book.

William Browne
B.M. M.S. Lansdown Collection No. 777 (1650)
pub. Brydges (1815)

Here six foot deep in his fast sleep
    The Lord of Lampasse lies,
Who his end made, with his own blade,
    Betwixt his mistress thighs;
If through that hole to heav'n he stole
    I dare be bold to say,
He was the first which that way past,
    And the last which found the way.

Anon   *Witt's Interpreter* (1655)

AN EPITAPH ON NIOBE TURN'D TO STONE

This Pile thou see'st, built out of Flesh not Stone,
Contains no Shroud within, nor moulding Bone:

This Blood-less Trunk is destitute of Tomb,
Which may the Soul-fled Mansion enwomb.

This seeming Sepulchre (to tell the troth)
Is neither Tomb, nor Body; and yet Both.

Henry King   *Poems, Elegies, Paradoxes and Sonnets* (1657)

AN EPITAPH FOR A WICKED MAN'S TOMB

Here lies the carcass of a cursèd sinner,
Doomed to be roasted for the devil's dinner.

Robert Wild   d. 1679   Hunt, *Poems by Robert Wilde* (1870)

ON THE DEATH OF KING CHARLES

WRITTEN WITH THE POINT OF HIS SWORD

Great! Good! and Just! Could I but rate
My griefs, and thy too rigid fate,
I'd sweep the world to such a strain
As it should deluge once again.
But since my loud-tongu'd blood demands supplies
More from Briareus' hands than Argus' eyes,
I'll sing thy obsequies with trumpet sounds,
And write thy epitaph with blood and wounds.

James Graham, the Marquis of Montrose
Winstanley, *England's Worthies* (1684)

FOR MY OWN TOMB-STONE

To Me 'twas giv'n to die: to Thee 'tis giv'n
To live: Alas! one Moment sets us ev'n.
Mark! how impartial is the Will of Heav'n?

Matthew Prior   *Poems on Several Occasions* (1718)

LORD CONINGSBY'S EPITAPH

Here lies Lord Coningsby – be civil!
The rest God knows – so does the devil!

Alexander Pope   written c. 1729 *Miscellanies* (1732)
from the Latin

EPITAPH FOR ISAAC NEWTON*

Nature and Nature's Laws lay hid in Night.
God said *Let Newton be*! and all was Light.

Alexander Pope   Lewis, *Miscellany* (1730)

EPITAPH

Here Delia's buried at Fourscore:
When *young*, a lewd, rapacious Whore,
Vain, and expensive; but when *old*,
A pious, sordid, drunken Scold.

Hildebrand Jacob   *Works* (1735)

* See No. 693

EPIGRAM UPON A FAT FELLOW

I
Stop Friend, and see,
What yet may be,
In Future Ages heard;
In doleful wise,
Here under lies,
A Ton of Guts inter'd.

II
Earth, lie thou light,
Upon the Wight,
For sure he was thy brother;
 Then shall the Crow,
  Have Puddings, so
And one Hog root another.

John Winstanley *Poems* (1742)

(PARODY ON AN EPITAPH SEEN IN THE LAKE DISTRICT)

Now clean, now hideous, mellow now, now gruff,
She swept, she hiss'd, she ripen'd & grew rough,
At Broom, Pendragon, Appleby & Brough.

Thomas Gray
written 1767 Gosse, *Works in Prose and Verse* (1884)

ON THE TOMB STONE OF A MAN WHO HAD A REMARKABLE LARGE MOUTH

Here lies a man, as God shall me save,
Whose mouth was wide as in his grave:
Reader tread lightly o'er his clod,
For if he wakes you're gone by G–d!

Anon   *A collection of Poems, Epigrams etc.*
Extracted from Newspapers (1770–95?)

EPITAPH ON ORTHON, WHO DIED DRUNK

Thus Orthon cries – My fate, ye Topers, mark,
And travel not, top-heavy in the Dark!
Drunk on the Road I died! How hard my Doom –
For Heaps of native Earth, a foreign Tomb!

Richard Polwhele
The Idyllia, Epigrams and Fragments of Theocritus (1786)
From the Greek of Theocritus

EPITAPH ON DOCTOR JOHNSON

Here lies poor Johnson : reader have a care,
Tread lightly, lest you rouse a sleeping bear –
Religious, moral, generous, and humane
He was – but self sufficient, rude and vain,
Ill bred, and overbearing in dignity,
A scholar and a christian – yet a brute;
Would you know all his wisdom and his folly,
His actions, sayings, mirth, and melancholy,
Boswell and Thrale, retailers of his wit,
Will tell you how he wrote, and talked, and coughed and spit.

Soame Jenyms   *Gentleman's Magazine* (1786)

ON A NOTED COXCOMB

(CAPTAIN WILLIAM RODDICK OF CORBISTON)

'Light lay the earth on Billy's breast,'
  His chicken heart so tender;
But build a castle on his head,
  His skull will prop it under.

Robert Burns   written 1793 *Glenriddel MS*

(ON A SUICIDE)

Here lies in earth a root of Hell
   Set by the Deil's ain dibble:
This worthless body damn'd himsel
   To save the Lord the trouble.

Robert Burns   written 1795–6
Stewart, *Poems Ascribed to Robert Burns* (1802)

An excellent adage commands that we should
Relate of the dead that alone which is good;
But of the great Lord who here lies in lead
We know nothing good but that he is dead.

Samuel Taylor Coleridge   *The Friend* (9 November 1809)

A NAMELESS EPITAPH

This sentence have I left behind
An aching body, and a mind
Not wholly blind,
Too keen to rest, too weak to find,
That travails sore, and brings forth wind,
Are God's worst portion to mankind.

Matthew Arnold   *New Poems* (1867)

Friends, when I breathe no more (and 'tis well known
That I am principally skin and bone)
See that my urn this epitaph presents,
'Cupid to Pluto, with his compliments.'

Richard Garnett   *Idylls and Epigrams* (1869)
After the Greek of Meleager

EPITAPH ON A YOUNG LADY WHO
WAS BIRCHED TO DEATH

They laid her flat on a goosedown pillow,
And scourged her arse with twigs of willow,
Her bottom so white grew pink, then red,
Then bloody, then raw, and her spirit fled.

Anon   *Cythera's Hymnal* (1870)

ON THE TOMB OF EDWARD COURTENAY,
THIRD EARL OF DEVON

Hoe! Hoe! Hoe! who lies here?
I the good Earl of Devonshire:
With Maud, my wife to me full dear
We lived together fifty-five year.
What we gave, we have;
What we spent, we had;
What we left, we lost.

Tiverton 1419
Anon   Cheales, *Epigrams and Epitaphs* (1877)

EPITAPH

Here lies the amorous Fanny Hicks,
The scabbard of ten thousand pricks,
And if you wish to do her honour,
Pull out your cock, and piss upon her.

Anon   *The Pearl* No. 5 (November 1879)

Here lies a man who never did
Anything but what he was bid;
Who lived his life in paltry ease,
And died of commonplace disease.

Robert Louis Stevenson   Colvin, *Letters* (1899)

BOMBED IN LONDON

On land and sea I strove with anxious care
To escape conscription. It was in the air!

COMMON FORM

If any question why we died,
Tell them, because our fathers lied.

A DEAD STATESMAN

I could not dig: I dared not rob:
Therefore I lied to please the mob.
Now all my lies are proved untrue
And I must face the men I slew.
What tale shall serve me here among
Mine angry and defrauded young?

Rudyard Kipling   *The Years Between* (1919)

MEMORIAL TO D. C. (VASSAR COLLEGE 1918)

I

Epitaph

Heap not on this mound
Roses that she loved so well;
Why bewilder her with roses,
That she cannot see or smell?

She is happy where she lies
With the dust upon her eyes.

EPITAPH ON AN ARMY OF MERCENARIES

These, in the day when heaven was falling,
The hour when earth's foundations fled,
Followed their mercenary calling
And took their wages and are dead.

Their shoulders held the sky suspended;
　　They stood, and earth's foundations stay;
What God abandoned, these defended,
　　And saved the sum of things for pay.

A. E. Housman　*Last Poems* (1922)

IN CONTINUATION OF POPE ON NEWTON

It did not last : the Devil howling 'Ho,
Let Einstein be,' restored the status quo.

J. C. Squire　*Poems* (1926)

LORD BEAVERBROOK

His epitaph : *He never ran unplaced;*
The world his oyster, though its pearls be paste;
And when, with all his 'ads' in front, he died
His trumpets sounded on the farther side.

Hubert Phillips　*A Diet of Crisps* (1929)

Here dead lie we because we did not choose
　　To live and shame the land from which we sprung.
Life, to be sure, is nothing much to lose;
　　But young men think it is, and we were young.

A. E. Housman　*More Poems* (1936)

EPITAPH FOR A DRUG-ADDICT

Mourn this young girl. Weep for society
Which gave her little to esteem but kicks.
Impatient of its code, cant, cruelty,
Indifference, she kicked against all pricks
But the dream-loaded hypodermic's. She
Has now obtained an everlasting fix.

Cecil Day Lewis   *The Whispering Roots* (1970)

SEXUAL

AGAINST A MAIDENLY MAN

For to be married yesterday,
To Church a gallant jetted gay:
His crisped locks wav'd all behind,
His tongue did lisp, his visage shind.
His roving eyes rold to and fro
He fisking fine did mincing go.
His lips and painted seemed sweet:
When as the Priest came them to meet,
(A pleasant scouse, though nought of life)
He askt of both which was the wife?

> Timothe Kendall   *Flowres of Epigrammes* (1577)
> After the Latin of Theodore Beza

IN KATUM

Kate being pleased, wisht that her pleasure could,
Endure as long as a buff jerkin would.
Content thee Kate, although thy pleasure wasteth,
Thy pleasures place like a buff jerkin lasteth:
  For no buff jerkin hath oftener worn,
   Nor hath more scrapings or more dressings born.

> Sir John Davies   *Epigrammes and Elegies* (159–?)

IN FRANCUM

When Francus comes to solace with his whore
He sends for rods and strips himself stark naked:
For his lust sleeps, and will not rise before,
By whipping of the wench it be awaked.
   I envy him not, but wish I had the power,
   To make myself his wench but one half hour.

                Sir John Davies   *Epigrammes and Elegies* (159–?)

  'Out of sight out of mind': this lie they mark,
  That lie with their drabs all night in the dark.

John Davies of Hereford   *Descant Upon English Proverbs* (1611)

IGNOTA, NULLA CUPIDO*

Florella, fal'n a year before her time,
(To salve the forfeit of her Maidenhead
That must no longer for promotion climb)
Prostrates herself unto a Viniter's bed,
   Where Gallants knock each midnight at her door,
   To taste the Juice that had no Bush before.

                Henry Parrot   *Laquei Ridiculosi* (1613)

* To no woman is desire unknown

AGAINST AN OLD LECHER

Since thy third curing of the French infection,
Priapus hath in thee found no erection,
Yet eat'st thou Ringoes, and Potato roots,
And Caviar, but it little boots.
Besides the bed's head a bottle's lately found,
Of liquor that a quart cost twenty pound:
For shame, if not more grace, yet shew more wit,
Surcease, now sin leaves thee, to follow it.
  Some smile, I sigh, to see thy madness such
  That that which stands not, stands thee in so much.

Sir John Harington
The Most Elegant and Wittie Epigrams (1618)

UPON SCOBBLE

Scobble for Whoredom whips his wife; and cries,
He'll slit her nose; But blubb'ring she replies,
Good Sir, make no more cuts i'th'outward skin,
One slit's enough to let Adultry in.

Robert Herrick   *Hesperides* (1648)

TO A LASCIVIOUS BLACKAMOOR WOMAN

'Tis Night in thine, in my face day: but yet
Should we join; we might mongrel twilight get;
A Tawny-moor that would of both partake;
Haunt me not Shade! I'll no new monster make.

Robert Heath   *Clarastella* (1650)

THE CHOICE OF HIS MISTRESS

I would not have a wench with such a waist
As might be well with a Thumb-Ring embrac'd;
Whose bony Hips, which out on both sides stick,
Might serve for Graters, and whose lean Knees prick;
One, which a saw does in her back-bone bear,
And in her Rump below carries a Spear.
Nor would I have her yet of bulk so gross
That weigh'd should break the scales at th' Market-cross;
A mere unfathom'd lump of Grease; no, that
Like they that will; 'tis Flesh I love, not Fat.

Edward Sheburne   *Salmacis* (1651)
After the Latin of Martial

THE WORDS OF ONE THAT WAS BOTH
A GREAT DRINKER AND A WENCHER,
IN EXCUSE OF BOTH

It is not for the love of drink, that I
Carouse so much; but for the company:
No more than it is for the nuptial cranny
That I grimbetilollelize my Jany;
It be'ng her belly, thigh, eyes, arms, mouth, face,
And other such appurtenances, as
    Accompany the integrants, that do it,
    Which so bewitchingly entice me to it.

Anon   *Ex Ungue Leonem* (1654)

ON MEETING A GENTLEWOMAN IN THE DARK

To see such dainty ghosts as you appear
Will make my flesh stand sooner than my hair.

Anon   *Wit's Interpreter* (1655)

NELL GWYNNE

Hard by Pall Mall lives a wench call'd Nell
    King Charles the Second he kept her.
She hath got a trick to handle his p—,
    But never lays hands on his sceptre.
All matters of state from her soul she does hate,
    And leaves to the politic bitches.
The whore's in the right, for 'tis her delight
    To be scratching just where it itches.

Anon
*The Second Part of the Collection of
Poems on Affairs of State* (1689)

UPON A TORY LADY WHO HAPPEN'D TO OPEN HER FLOODGATES AT THE TRAGEDY OF CATO

Whilst maudlin Whigs deplore their Cato's fate
Still with dry eyes the Tory Celia sate:
But tho' her Pride forbade her Eyes to flow,
The gusting Waters found a vent below,
Tho' secret, yet with copious Streams she mourns,
Like twenty River-Gods with all their Urns.
Let others screw a Hypocritic face,
She shows her Grief in a sincerer place!
Her Nature reigns, and Passion void of Art,
For this Road leads directly to the Heart.

Edward Ward(?)   *The Poetical Entertainer No. V* (1713)

The Crab does oft the tufted Ring possess,
And crawls unseen about the heavenly Place;
From whose soft Banks the whizing Waters fall,
And show'rs of Love perform the Dev'l and all.
But when old Time has stretch'd the Channel wide,
And stop'd the flux of the refresting Tide,
'Tis Drudg'ry then in such a Pool to Sail,
One moment makes us glad to say, *Farewell*.

Thomas Brown   *Works* (1715)

ON JOSEPH'S REFUSING POTIPHAR'S WIFE

For righteousness, to Joseph some impute
His cold denial of his lady's suit;
If we consider rightly, 'twill appear,
Th' Egyptians are not like our Ladies here;
Had he been sold into more Northern Climes,
Or liv'd a servant in these modern times,
Maugre his seeming Sanctity, you'd find,
He'd not have fled, and left his Coat behind.

Anon   *The Honey Suckle* (1734)

ON WOMAN

A Woman, tho' her Mouth be small,
Will sure take in the Devil and all;
Her Hands tho' little, Body spare,
She's large, and fat enough elsewhere.

Anon   *The Bath, Bristol, Tunbridge and Epsom Miscellany* (1735)

ON THE PICTURE OF SUSANNA

Susanna's Fate with Pity we behold,
Condemn'd to Lechers, impotent and old:
With wond'rous Art, the Pencil shews she fears
The faint Addresses – not the Force of Years.

Anon   *Joe Miller's Jests* (1742)

TO A LADY WHO MARRIED HER FOOTMAN

Dear cousin think it no reproach;
   (Thy virtue shines the more)
To take black John into the coach
   He rode *behind before*.

Anon   *Joe Miller's Jests* (1742)

LADY H— TO MRS P—

Said old Lady H—, once a blooming young wench,
   But whose head's now adorn'd with gray hairs,
'I admire the great comfort and taste which the French
   Combine in their fashions of chairs;
For English, our frames are both simple and neat;
   Yet the French in past times were so puff'd,
That our bottoms were never considered complete,
   Until sent o'er to France to be stuff'd.'

Anon   *Hilaria* (1798)

ON AN OLD WOMAN IN LOVE

For shame, Canidia! quit this itch to lust;
Thy sixtieth year rebukes thy tottering dust.
Your eyes to sparkle and your veins to glow
Now age o'er ev'ry look has spread her snow,
Forbear, old trull! Thus hoary Aetna lies,
Fleec'd with the winter of Sicilian skies;
Emblem of thee, her summit cap't with snow,
Seems to deny the raging fires below.

Anon   *The Spirit of the Public Journals for 1800*

'THE HARP THAT ONCE —'

The prick that once through Fanny's drawers,
   The soul of fucking shed,
Now hangs as mute as these two balls,
   As if that soul were dead.

My penis now so seldom stands,
   The only throb it gives,
Is when I rub it in my hands,
   To prove that still it lives.

          Anon   *The Cremorne* No. 1 (January 1851)

AMEN

Oh! cunt is a kingdom, and prick is its lord;
A whore is a slave, and her mistress a bawd;
Her quim is her freehold, which brings in her rent
Where you pay when you enter, and leave when you've spent.

          Anon   *The Pearl* No. 1   (July 1879)

EPIGRAM ON PRIAPUS

Why laugh such laughter, O most silly maid?
My form Praxiteles nor Scopas hewed:
To me no Phidian handwork finish gave;
But me a bailiff hacked from shapeless log,
And quoth my maker 'Thou Priapus be!'
Yet on me gazing forthright gigglest thou
And holdest funny matter to deride
The pillar perking from the groin of me.

> Anon   *Priapeia* Cosmopolis (1890)

EPITAPH FOR OSCAR WILDE

Earth to earth, sod to sod,
That's how Oscar greets his God.
It was for sinners such as this
That God made Hell bottomless.

> attrib. to Charles Algernon Swinburne (1900?)

Boys, by girls held in their thighs
Shudder, and turn back their eyes.
It is as well they never see
The brute approach of ecstasy.

John Peale Bishop   written c. 1928 *Collected Poems* (1948)

NO! MR LAWRENCE

No, Mr Lawrence, it's not like that!
I don't mind telling you
I know a thing or two about love,
Perhaps more than you do.

And what I know is that you make it
too nice, too beautiful.
It's not like that, you know; you fake it.
It's really rather dull.

D. H. Lawrence *Pansies* (1929)

red rag and pink flag
blackshirt and brown
strut-mince and stink-brag
have all come to town

some like it shot
some like it hung
and some like it in the twot
nine months young

e. e. cummings *50 Poems* (1940)

Extensive and painful researches
By Darwin and Huxley and Hall
Have conclusively shown that the hedgehog
Can scarcely be buggered at all.

In the course of these painful researches
At Harvard and Princeton and Yale
They found that the ass of the hedgehog
Could be spiked with a ten penny nail.

Further extensive researches
Have incontrovertibly shown
That comparative safety at Harvard
Is enjoyed by the hedgehog alone.

Anon   *Folk Poems and Ballads* Mexico City (1945)

Gather ye rosebuds while ye may,
Old time is still a-flying.
And the pecker which is stiff today
Tomorrow will be dying.

Anon   *Folk Poems and Ballads* Mexico City (1945)

PICCADILLY

At the hub of Empire little Eros stands
Warming his testicles in chilly hands;
They dare not take him down before
They pass the anti-masturbation law.
But when at last the nation's purity
Is one day locked in firm security
They'll shift the Roman exile for to be
The patron saint of our psychiatry.

Lawrence Durrell   written 1958 *Collected Poems* (1974)

ALDPORT

(MYSTERY TOUR)

Hearing how tourists, dazed with reverence
Look through sunglasses at the Parthenon
Dai thought of that cold night outside the Gents
When he touched Dilys up with his gloves on.

Kingsley Amis   *A Look Around the Estate* (1967)

Sotades' head is in the noose.
How come? Who would accuse
So upright and so straight a man?
He's under a different sort of ban –
a pity a chap who's so well-hung
has to rely upon his tongue.

Peter Porter   *After Martial* (1972)
After the Latin of Martial

I can remember, Lesbia, when you swore
You were mine and mine only, called me more
Desirable than Jove. I loved you then,
And not just in the way that other men
Love mistresses, but as a father cares
For his own sons and daughters, for his heirs.
Now that I know you, you're much cheaper, lighter,
And yet desire in me flares even brighter.
'How can that be?' you say. In love deceit
Freezes affection, though it stokes up heat.

James Michie   *The Poems of Catullus* (1972)
After the Latin of Catullus

THE IMPOTENT LOVER

You send for her, you tell her to come, you get everything
    ready,
    but if anyone really comes, what will you
get up to? Think how things stand with you, Automedon:
    The cock that was spirited and stiff is dead now
and shrivelled between your legs. How they'll laugh if you
    put to sea empty handed, an oarsman who's lost his oar.

W. S. Merwin   *The Greek Anthology* (1973)
After the Greek of Automedon

Mademoiselle Desirée lounges in front of me on the champs
    fête grass
stark naked save for her net stockings, fashionable Parisian legs
    crossed,
twiddling her left nipple as she squirms on her arse:
I stare into her green Pigalle eyes and I am lost.

What I cannot see as I devour this delicious Morgan
le Fay is the set of tigershark teeth located
invisibly within the lips of her sexual organ
like a carnivorous mantrap deliciously set and baited.

George Barker   *In Memory of David Archer* (1973)

The bath–house bench pinched Graphicus' bottom.
So even a plank has feelings, and I'm a man . . .

W. G. Shepherd   *The Greek Anthology* (1973)
After the Greek of Strato

179

Time was when once upon a time, such toys
As balls or pet birds won a boy, or dice.
Now its best china, or cash. Lovers of boys
Try something else next time. Toys cut no ice.

Peter Jay   *The Greek Anthology* (1973)
After the Greek of Glaukos

SOCIAL

The humour of Tobacco (and the rest)
    Wherein our gallants took their chief delight:
Is daily had (methinks) in less request,
    And will (I fear) in time be worn out quite.
For now each peasant puffs it through the nose:
As well as he that's clad in velvet hose.

                  Henry Parrot   *The Mous-Trap* (1606)

A Welshman and an Englishman disputed,
Which of their lands maintain'd the greatest state;
The Englishman the Welshman quite confuted,
Yet would the Welshman nought his brags abate.
    Ten cooks (quoth he) in Wales one wedding sees:
    True, quoth the other, each man toasts his cheese.

                  Henry Parrot   *Laquei Ridiculosi* (1613)

UPON A PROUD PAINTED UPSTART LADY

What makes that painted puppet stand for th' wall?
If you would know the cause quoth one, you shall.
Her father was a Mason as men say,
Which makes her Ladyship still lean that way.
Beshrew my dim dull eyes, for now I see
In both her cheeks written her pedigree;
Her nose is like a Trowel, and her Chin
A Tray such as they carry mortar in.
Walk on good lime and hair, I ever shall
As duty binds, give to thy wall the wall.

John Eliot   *Poems* (1658)

(ON LOPPING TREES IN HIS GARDEN)

My Lord complains, that Pope, stark mad with gardens,
Has lopt three trees the value of three farthings:
But he's my neighbour, cries the peer polite,
And if he'll visit me, I'll wave my right.
What? on Compulsion? and against my Will,
A Lord's acquaintance? Let him file his Bill.

Alexander Pope   written c. 1740   (1741)

AN EPIGRAM ON SCOLDING

Great Folks are of a finer Mold;
Lord! how politely they can scold;
While a coarse English Tongue will itch,
For Whore and Rogue; and Dog and Bitch.

Jonathan Swift   *Works* Dublin (1746)

FROM THE FRENCH

That all from Adam first begun,
  Sure none but Whiston doubts;
And that his son, and his son's son,
  Were plowmen, clowns, and louts.

Here lies the only diff'rence now,
  Some shot off late, some soon;
Your sires in the morning left off plough,
  And ours in th' afternoon.

Jonathan Swift(?) *The Poetical Farrago* (1794)

When two persons discover that they have a passion in
  common,
  Sex, Donizetti or Chows, Class is no barrier at all:
Secret to every class, though, its code of polite conversation,
  How one should carry on when talking to strangers and
  bores.

W. H. Auden *Epistle to a Godson* (1972)

GLASGOW SCHOOLBOYS,
RUNNING BACKWARDS

Highwind . . . They turn their backs to it, and push.
Their crazy strides are chopped in little steps.
And all their lives, like that, they'll have to rush
Forwards in reverse, always holding their caps.

Douglas Dunn *Barbarians* (1979)

SOPHISTICAL

ON GUT

Gut eats all day, and lechers all the night,
  So all his meat he tasteth over, twice:
And striving so to double his delight,
  He makes himself a thorough-fare of vice.
Thus, in his belly, can he change a sin
  Lust it comes out, that gluttony went in.

Ben Jonson   Workes (1616)

OF MAURUS HIS ORPHEUS – LIKE MELODY

Maurus, last morn, at's mistress window played
An Hunts-up on his lute : but she, (it's said)
Threw stones at him : so he, like Orpheus, there,
Made stones come flying his sweet notes to hear.

John Davies of Hereford   Wit's Bedlam (1617)

A LAME BEGGAR

I am unable, yonder beggar cries
To stand, or move; if he say true, he lies.

John Donne   Poems (1633)

IN THE MOTION OF THE STARS

Artists affirm that from the burning Line,
Some Stars of Aries North-ward now decline,
And the slow-pac'd Cynosure appears
Nearer the fixt pole, than in former years
No marvel then blind mortals walk astray,
When Heaven's clear eyes have lost their wonted way.

Thomas Bancroft
Two Books of Epigrammes and Epitaphs (1639)

THE NEW WORLD

Some in the Moon another world have found,
Whose brighter parts are Seas, the darker, Ground:
Which were it true, we would have Moon-Calves tost
From those sharp whirling Horns to every Coast:
And a wild World it were, and full of tricks,
Where all Inhabitants were Lunatics.

Thomas Bancroft
Two Books of Epigrammes and Epitaphs (1639)

UPON THE WEIGHTS OF A CLOCK

I wonder time's so swift, when as I see
Upon her heels, such lumps of lead to be.

Anon   *Witt's Recreations* (1640)

A LIE, AND NO LIE

'Tis not still out of sight and out of mind,
For one may mind his meat that is stark blind:
But he that's blind, and hath no mind to eat,
Then out of sight and mind, is that man's meat.

John Taylor *Epigrammes* (1651)

TO HIS UNCONSTANT MISTRESS

Satan, no woman, yet a wandering spirit,
   Once did hell disinherit
   O'th Sailor's Trade,
   (By strict inquiry made)
When he saw ships sail two ways with one wind.
The Devil himself, loves not a wavering mind.

Samuel Sheppard *Epigrams* (1651)

OF VIR, IN VIRGINITY

Dem.

Why, hath the word Virginity, Vir in't;
Seeing maids (as such) ply not t'a a virile dint?

Answ.
Because the Moon within her hath a Man,
And yet's a virgin, call'd the chaste Diane.

Anon *Ex Ungue Leonem* (1654)

ON WOMEN

A woman may be fair, and yet her mind
Is as constant as the wavering wind:
Venus herself is fair, and shineth far
Yet she's a planet, and no fixed star.

Anon   *Wit's Interpreter* (1655)

O Love! What Pains do I endure?
  Have Patience, Swain, they'll soon be pass'd,
Your very Passion brings its Cure,
Since all Philosophers assure,
  Nothing that's violent, can last.

Hildebrand Jacob   *Works* (1735)

'WORDS ARE BUT WIND' – TALE OF A TUB

If Words are Wind, as some allow,
  No Promises can bind,
Since breaking of the strictest Vow,
  Is only breaking Wind.

Stephen Duck   *Poems on Several Occasions* (1736)

If the Man who Turnips cries
Cry not when his Father dies;
'Tis a Sign that he had rather
Have a Turnip than a Father.

Samuel Johnson   *The Westminster Magazine* (September 1774)
From the Spanish of Lope de Vega

A RAKE'S ECONOMY

With cards and dice, and dress and friends,
    My savings are complete;
I light the candle at both ends,
    And thus make both ends meet.

Anon   *The Jest Book* (1864)

WHY THE SEA IS SALT

Why was the sea made salt? Because, I think,
If fresh, the fishes every drop would drink.

F. P. Barnard   *A Fardel of Epigrams* (1922)
From the Latin of Timothy Polus

DEAN SWIFT WATCHES SOME COWS

How, when they lift their Tails, the Shit shoots out!
A foul Volcanoe next a Waterspout.
The Anus and Vagina are so near,
Each lovely Dame cannot repress a Tear
To think she's modelled on the selfsame Pattern.
And so are Queens, and so is ev'ry Slattern.

'Twas the Propinquity of these two Holes
That made Divines doubt Women had not Souls.
They knew those Furrows that would bear the Tilth –
Men could not choose but sow their Seed in Filth –
And how from Ordure sprung could Life be good
Or Mystery be part of Womanhood?

       Gavin Ewart   *The Gavin Ewart Show* (1971)

SPIRITUAL

The Sun which shines amid the heaven so bright
And guides our eyes to heaven by his light:
Will not be gazed on of a fleshly eye.
But blinds that sight which dares to see so high:
   Even he doth tell us that heaven doth require
   Far better eyes of them which would see higher.

             Thomas Bastard   *Chrestoleros* (1598)

  Of God, but by God none can think aright.
  As none can see the light, but by the light.

        John Heath   *Two Centuries of Epigrams* (1610)

  What we of Christ, but by tradition hear,
  That to the Jews did visibly appear:
  And therefore did they not believe, I ween
  For faith it is of things which are not seen.

        John Heath   *Two Centuries of Epigrams* (1610)

OF THE CORN THAT RAINED

I handled, tasted, saw it with mine eyes,
The grain that lately fell down from the skies;
Yet what it tok'ned could I not devise,
And many doubts did in my mind arise.
At last, I thus resolv'd, it signifies
   That this is our sole mean, to mend this dearth.
   To ask from heav'n, that we do lack on earth.

Sir John Harington
The Most Elegant and Wittie Epigrams &c (1618)

UPON ST THOMAS, HIS UNBELIEF

Faith comes by hearsay, love by sight: then he
May well believe, and love whom he doth see:
But since men leave both hope, and charity,
And faith is made the greatest of the three,
All doctrine goes for truth: then say I thus,
More goes to heaven with Thomas Didymus.

Sir John Suckling   *Cranfield Papers, MS* (c. 1626)

HOMO

Man's like the *Earth*, his *hair* like *grass* is grown,
His *Veins* the *Rivers* are, his *Heart* the *Stone*.

John Pyne   *Epigrammata Officiosa, Religiosa, Iocosa* (1627)

ON AFFLICTION

When thou afflict'st me, Lord, if I repine,
I show myself to be mine own, not thine.

Francis Quarles   *Divine Fancies* (1632)

The Hebrews at the sacred fountains quaft,
The Grecians at the rivers take their draft,
The Latins at the silver brooks do drink,
English, and others, at the lakes' small brink.

Edward May   *Epigrams Divine and Morall* (1633)

Earth is an Island ported round with Fears;
The way to Heav'n is through the Sea of tears.
It is a stormy passage, where is found
The wrack of many a ship, but no man drown'd.

Francis Quarles   *Emblemes* (1635)

ON THE MIRACLE OF MULTIPLIED LOAVES

See here an easy Feast that knows no wound,
    That under Hungers Teeth will needs be sound:
A subtle Harvest of unbounded bread,
    What would ye more? Here food it self is fed.

Richard Crashaw   *Steps to the Temple* (1646)

ETERNITY

O Years! and Age! Farewell:
   Behold I go,
   Where I do know
Infinity to dwell.

And these mine eyes shall see
   All times, how they
   Are lost i'th'Sea
Of vast Eternity.

Where never Moon shall sway
   The Stars; but she,
   And Night, shall be
Drown'd in one endless Day.

        Robert Herrick   *His Noble Numbers* (1648)

God, whom no time confines, oft stays, to save,
Till hope and help, from all things else, are fled;
That so his work may the more glory have
Christ did not come, till Lazarus was dead.

        Henry Delaune   *ΠΑΤΡΙΚΟΝ ΔΩRON* (1657)

The World's a Prison; no man can get out:
Let th'Atheist storm then; 'tis Heav'n round about.

        Barten Holyday   *A Survey of the World* (1661)

ON ANATOMY

Subtract Church and his Members, holy ones,
The world is nothing but a trunk of bones.

Nicholas Billingsley   *A Treasury of Divine Raptures* (1667)

OF GOD

In Vain we seek to know what God is since
He's a vast Circle whose Circumference
Is nowhere, and his Centre everywhere;
Where e'er we seek him there, we find him there;
But what he is, he were not *God*, if he
By human thought cou'd comprehended be.
Go seek the Heavens above, th' Abyss below,
And World about, and all these we may know,
But God, who nor beginning has, nor end,
How can we know? How can we comprehend?
Well then did that Philosopher of Old
Who did the Ebb and Flow o'th'sea behold;
And restlessly did seek to comprehend
The reason of it, thus cry out i'th'end:
Since I can't comprehend thee, thou at least
Comprehend me; and I shall be at rest.

Richard Flecknoe
A Collection of the Choicest Epigrams and Characters (1673)

EPIGRAM ON PRAYER

Prayer highest soars when she most prostrate lies,
And when she supplicates, she storms the skies.
Thus to gain Heav'n may seem an easy task,
For what can be more easy than to ask?
Yet oft we do and by sad experience find,
That, clogged with earth, some prayers are left behind,
And some like chaff blown off by every wind.
To kneel is easy, to pronounce not hard,
Then why are some petitions debarr'd?
Hear what an ancient oracle declared;
Some *sing* their prayers, and some their prayers *say*,
He's an Elias, who his prayers can pray.
    Reader, remember, when you next repair
    To church or closet, this memoir of prayer.

Anon   *The Monitor* (March 1713)

ON ST PAULS

This is God's House; but 'tis to be deplor'd,
More come to see the house than serve its Lord.

Anon   *Epigrams in Distich* (1740)

THE WATER TURNED TO WINE

When Christ, at Cana's feast, by pow'r divine,
Inspir'd cold water with the warmth of wine,
See! cried they, while, in red'ning tide, it gush'd,
The bashful stream hath seen its God, and *blush'd*.

Aaron Hill   *Works* (1753)
From the Latin of Richard Crashaw

It fortifies my soul to know
That, though I perish, Truth is so;
That, howsoe'er I stray and range,
Whate'er I do, thou dost not change.
I steadier step when I recall
That, if I slip, thou dost not fall.

A. H. Clough   *Poems* (1862)
From the German of Goethe

'Faith' is a fine invention
When Gentlemen can *see* –
But *Microscopes* are prudent
In an Emergency.

Emily Dickinson   written c.1860 *Poems by Emily Dickinson*
Second Series (1891)

ON A SUNDIAL

Here in a lonely glade, forgotten, I
Mark the tremendous process of the sky.
So does your inmost soul, forgotten, mark
The Dawn, the Noon, the coming of the Dark.

Hilaire Belloc   *Sonnets and Verse* (1938)

THEOLOGICAL

OF GOING TO HEAVEN AND HELL

Of heaven or of hell, which go folk fastest to?
To hell, fool, to hell go far more fast they do.
The high way to both lieth thus as clerks tell,
Uphill to heavenward, downhill to hell.

John Heywood   *Workes* (1562)

IN ADORANTES RELIQUIAES*

Is it a worthy thing to dig up bones?
To kiss, t'adore the relics of dead men?
Alas how foolish were those silly ones,
Which in times past did nought but bury them?
But they perhaps for stink did then refrain:
But you do worse to make them stink again.
    Yet in the very stinking this is odd.
    They stank to men then, now they stink to God.

Thomas Bastard   *Chrestoleros* (1598)

* On those who worship relics.

A PURITAN

Dame Lais is a puritan by religion,
Impure in her deeds, though pure in her talk,
And therefore a puritan by condition,
or pluritan, which after many doth walk;
for prurity of women, by lecherous direction,
seeks plurity of men to work satisfaction.

Francis Thynne   *Emblemes and Epigrames* (1600)

IN TRANSUBSTANTIATORES*

The Cannibals eat men with greediness:
And Transubstantiors do no less:
No less? nay more; and that far more by odds;
Those eat man's flesh, these ravine upon God's.

John Heath   *Two Centuries of Epigrames* (1610)

It is an Art beyond the work of Nature,
The Pope should be Creator, and a creature:
Betwixt the Pope and God there's one thing odd,
For though God all things made, the Pope makes God.

John Taylor   *The Sculler* (1612)

* On the Transubstantiators

OF DEATH

He that fears death, or mourns it, in the just,
Shows of the Resurrection little trust.

Ben Jonson *Workes* (1616)

OF READING SCRIPTURES

The sacred Scripture treasure great affords,
To all of several tongues, of sundry Realms.
For low and simple spirits shallow Fords,
For high and learned Doctors deeper streams,
In every part so exquisitely made,
An Elephant may swim, a lamb may wade.
Not that all should with barbarous audacity,
Read what they list, or how they list expound,
But each one suiting to his weak capacity:
For many great Scriptureans may be found,
That cite Saint Paul at every bench and board,
And have God's word, but have not God the word.

Sir John Harington
The Most Elegant and Wittie Epigrams (1618)

UPON THE TURKISH ALKARON

The Turks hold this opinion very odd,
That madmen's souls are talking still with God,
And that to be an Idiot or a Vice,
Is th'only way to purchase Paradise:
   If this be true that Alkaron's relate,
   Our Puritans were sure in happy state.

Henry Peacham   *Thalia's Banquet* (1620)

TO A CURIOUS QUESTIONER

Oft have you urg'd me earnestly to tell
Wheth'r Earth or Air shall be the place of Hell.
Be not like Travellers; they desire to know
Where the place lies unto which they go.

John Pyne   *Epigrammata Officiosa, Religiosa, Iocosa* (1627)

POPERIES PRINCIPAL ABSURDITIES

Of all the hud-winkt tricks in Popery,
This is the lamentablest foppery:
When God is made to speak, and to command
Men, in a tongue they do not understand,
And Men commanded are to Sing and Pray
To such fond things that know not what they say,
And these men having madly, sadly pray'd,
Themselves do not know, what themselves have said.

Robert Hayman   *Quodlibets* (1628)

SIN

O That I could a sin once see!
We paint the devil foul, yet he
Hath some good in him, all agree.
Sin is flat opposite to th' Almighty, seeing
It wants the good of *vertue*, and of *being*.

But God more care of us hath had:
If apparitions make us sad,
By sight of sin we should grow mad.
Yet as in sleep we see foul death, and live:
So devils are our sins in perspective.

George Herbert   *The Temple* (1633)

EPIGRAM ON CALVIN

Calvin, in pay of that despairing sin
He laid on Christ, himself did die therein.
And while from forth his ulcerous flesh did burst,
Worms, stench, & lice, still swore, blasphem'd & curst,
And on the Devil without rest did call:
Which argueth his good nature, and that all
His wits were perfect, since so near his end
He had so clear remembrance of his friend.

Anon   *Mirrour of New Reformation* Paris (1634)

OF MORTIFICATION

Sith Paradise is lost, look not to see
God in soft pleasures walks : for surely he
That did to Moses in a Bush appear
Loves sharp compunction, and a life austere.

Thomas Bancroft
Two Bookes of Epigrammes and Epitaphs (1639)

ON THE POPE'S PORPHYRY CHAIR, WHEREIN THEY ARE GROUPED AND TRIED TO BE MAN

Popes need no Porphyry chair now for to try
If they be males or not; they it descry
To all the world before-hand by the store
Of Bastards they beget. It then were more
Fit now, their Testicles to cut, than grope,
For fear a Letcher, not a Whore, turn Pope.

William Prynne   *A Pleasant Purge for a Roman Catholike* (1642)

TO OUR LORD, UPON THE WATER MADE WINE

Thou water turn'st to Wine (fair friend of Life)
Thy foe to cross the sweet Arts of thy Reign
Distils from thence the Tears of wrath and strife,
And so turns wine to Water back again.

Richard Crashaw   *Steps to the Temple* (1646)

THE RESURRECTION POSSIBLE, AND PROBABLE

For each one Body, that i'th earth is sown,
There's an up-rising but of one for one:
But for each Grain, that in the ground is thrown,
Threescore or fourscore spring up thence for one:
So that the wonder is not half so great,
Of ours, as is the rising of the wheat.

Robert Herrick   *His Noble Numbers* (1648)

A PACIFICATION

By Moses Law, he that desir'd to take
His Captive to his bed, meaning to make
His slave his Wife, must clean cut off her hair,
Give her new garments, and her nails must pare:

So let the Church of Rome repudiate
Her Superfluities; find her pristine State,
We two will be one flesh, hate banisht quite,
She shall be unto us an Israelite.

Samuel Sheppard · *Epigrams* (1651)

OF KNOX THE SABBATARIAN

Knox makes no conscience of Adultery
Of Rapine, Theft, or Petty Larceny;
Yet hang'd his Cat for killing of a Mouse
Upon the Sabbath-day within his house.

Anon   *Ex Ungue Leonem* (1654)

203

A PESTILENT PROFEST PURITAN

I do believe that the accursed sect
Is much more ancient than men do suspect.
The Jews, when Christ was crucifi'd I find,
In that dam'd act, were variously inclin'd.
Some pierc't his side, others his name deride,
Another Crew his garments did divide.
And these were Puritans, I'll lay my life,
Whose seed since then have ever been at strife
With Surplices, with Rockets, and with Coaps,
Hating to hear of figures or of Tropes.
Real presence, and what's good by thems abated,
With brain sick Zeal more than the devil it's hated.
  Go on mad beasts put on our saviour's Coats
  But his bright Eyes will know his sheep from goats.

John Eliot   *Poems* (1658)

ON THE CRUCIFYING OF OUR SAVIOUR AND SAINT PETER

Christ's feet were down plac'd, Peter's up, which shows
Christ from the Cross descended, Peter rose.

James Wright   *Sales Epigrammatum* (1663)
From the Latin of Bernadus Bauhusius

ÆTHIOP'S LOTUS

How fair this Æthiop comes from th' holy fount?
To wash a Black we may not vain account.
How bright a Soul is in a cloudy skin!
The Dove now loves a black house to dwell in.

Clement Barksdale *Epigrammata Sacra Selecta* (1682)

ON THE AUTHOR OF THE HIND
AND PANTHER

To put religion into dogg'rel rhyme
May well befit the Trentists of our time;
For being naked found in holy writ
They fly for refuge to her fig-leaf'd wit.

Anon *Folger 4731* (1687)

THE TOBACCO SOT

Says Jack, a dry consumptive smoking sot,
Whose Mouth with Weed was always glowing hot,
Where shall I go, alas, when Death shall come,
And with his rawbon'd Clutches seal my Doom?
Faith, replies Tom, *there can no Heaven be,*
Without Tobacco, for such Sots as thee.
Nor need you fear a Hell when you expire,
You've dealt so much on Earth in Smoke and Fire.

Edward Ward(?) *The Poetical Entertainer No 3* (1712)

See how the wand'ring Danube flows,
    Realms and religion parting!
A friend to all true Christian foes,
    To Peter, Jack, and Martin.

Now Protestant, and Papist now;
    Not constant long to either;
At length an infidel does grow,
    And ends his journey neither.

Thus many a youth I've known set out,
    Half Protestant, half Papist
And rambling long the world about,
    Turn infidel and atheist.

        Jonathan Swift(?)   *The Christmas Treat* (1767)

SAWNEY'S COMFORT

Lord, what a goodly thing is want of shirts!
How a Scotch stomach, and no meat, converts!
We wanted food and raiment, so we took
Religion for a sempstress and a cook.

        Anon   written 1630 *The Poetical Farrago* (1794)

WRITTEN AT BATH

The church and rooms, the other day,
Open'd their books for pray'r and play:
The priest got six – Hoyle sixty seven;
How great the odds for Hell, 'gainst Heav'n!

        Anon   *The Poetical Farrago* (1794)

His noggin fill'd three parts of gin,
Tom puts but little water in;
And blam'd for this, the drunken lout
Answers you thus, with looks devout:–
'St Paul (and you'll allow him merit)
Expressly says – "*Quench not the Spirit*"!'

     Anon *The Spirit of the Public Journals for 1805*

Grown old in Love from Seven till Seven times Seven
I oft have wished for Hell for Ease from Heaven.

       William Blake *Notebook* 1807

(FOUND IN A BIBLE)

One day at least in every week,
 The sects of every kind,
Their doctrines here are sure to seek,
 And just as sure to find.

     Anon *Notes & Queries* (27 January 1855)
            From the Latin

Why should scribblers discompose
Our temper? would we look like those?
There are some curs in every street
Who snarl and snap at all they meet:
The taller mastiff deems it aptest
To lift a leg and play the baptist.

    Walter Savage Landor *Heroic Idylls* (1863)

CENSURE AND PRAISE

S. Peter by S. Paul is named,
And for his carnal conduct blamed:
S. Paul is in S. Peter's turn
Extolled for mysteries hard to learn.

Anon   *Epigrams Sacred and Moral* (1864)

A crowd of grave enquirers made resort,
To where the learned doctors held their court;
And asked them, who had been that serpent brute,
Which tempted mother Eve to eat the fruit?
'Ye silly men,' the sages did reply,
'Why do ye waste your time and ours, oh why?
Eve's tempting snake was but a long and thick,
Great, knotty, ruddy, massy, mighty prick!'

Anon   *The Pearl No. 17* (1880)

THINKERS, PAST AND PRESENT

God, by the earlier sceptic, was exiled;
The later is more lenient grown and mild:
He sanctions God provided you agree
To any other name for deity.

William Watson   *Epigrams of Art, Life and Nature* (1884)

LE CHRISTIANISME

So the church Christ was hit and buried
    Under its rubbish and its rubble.
In cellars, packed-up saints lie serried,
    Well out of hearing of our trouble.

One Virgin still immaculate
    Smiles on for war to flatter her.
She's halo'd with an old tin hat,
    But a piece of hell will batter her.

> Wilfred Owen   written 1917
> Blunden, *Poems* (1931)

ON AN OSTRICH AT THE EDINBURGH ZOO WHO SWALLOWED A COPY OF THE OLD TESTAMENT

Empty of human wile or wit
This act of faith he ne'er foresaw;
And lives – still innocent of it –
Upon the prophets and the law.

> William Soutar   *Brief Words* (1935)

Stars, I have seen them fall,
    But when they drop and die
No star is lost at all
    From all the star-sown sky.
The toil of all that be
    Helps not the primal fault;
It rains into the sea,
    And still the sea is salt.

A. E. Housman   *More Poems* (1936)

ON A PURITAN

He served his God so faithfully and well
That now he sees him face to face, in hell.

Hilaire Belloc   *Sonnets and Verse* (1938)

A LA REINE BLANCHE

Garçon, I will always remember certain dreams
Associated with your serving the petite mademoiselle
Un café au lait – for it was then you looked
Most like God when he fell in love
With Himself and Beauty and forgot his uglier clients.

Adil Jussawalla   *Lands End* (1962)

All things (e.g. a camel's journey through
A needle's eye) are possible, it's true.
But picture how the camel feels, squeezed out
In one long bloody thread from tail to snout.

C. S. Lewis   *Poems* (1964)

DEITIES AND BEASTS

Tall Atlas, Jupiter, Hercules, Thor
Just like the antic pagan gods of yore
Make up a too-erratic pantheon
For mortal men to be dependent on.

I much prefer, myself, the humble RAT,
The tiny Ferrier, the Short Hawk that
Makes secret flight, and the Sparrow whose fall
Is never mentioned in the press at all.

John Updike   *Verse* (1965)

HE

Slave to a god whose sole verb is *Flatter*!
His world a sceptre and his soul a wraith
Astray in the illusion he called *Matter*,
He got religion when he lost his faith.

Howard Nemerov   *The Western Approaches* (1975)

TOPOGRAPHICAL

THE CANARIES

Those Isles were wont to be call'd fortunate,
Have now their names Canaries, for the Curres
That breed therein (a Metamorphos'd state,
And strange) which thinks here blest for beastly Burres.
  But Britains Isle should certain more be blest,
  If with mad dogs she were the lesser prest.

William Gamage *Linsi-Woolsie* (1613)

TO ASIA

Blest Region, where my sacred Saviour walkt,
And God with Man in flowery Eden talkt,
I reverence thy soil, preferring thee,
The world's fourth part, before the other three,
Though vast America against my strain
Swell with proud hills of gold, and high disdain.

Thomas Bancroft
Two Books of Epigrammes and Epitaphs (1639)

ON PALESTINE

My sighs out-pace my tongue, when I would tell
How this fam'd Region, which did all excell
In pleasant fruits, and typ'd the happiest place,
Is now a den of barbarism, so base,
So stript and ruin'd, that with grapes and grain,
It scarce a flight of locusts can maintain.
Ah cursedness of sin, that thus to gall
Turns milk and honey, and empoisons all.

Thomas Bancroft
Two Books of Epigrammes and Epitaphs (1639)

TO HIS HOUSEHOLD GODS

Rise, Household Gods, and let us go;
But whither, I my self not know.
First, let us dwell on rudest seas;
Next, with severest Salvages;
Last, let us make our best abode,
Where human foot, as yet, ne'r trod:
Search worlds of Ice; and rather there
Dwell, than in loathèd Devonshire.

Robert Herrick   *Hesperides* (1648)

When Neptune saw the Walls of Venice stand
High on the Floods, and all the Sea command:
Now, Jove, said he, let no tarpeian Tow'rs,
Or Mars's Buildings, be compar'd with ours.
If you the Tiber to the Sea prefer,
Look on both cities, and you cannot err;
But must acknowledge, when you see the odds,
That yours were built by Men, and mine by Gods.

John Hanway
Translations of Several Odes, Satyrs & Epistles (1730)
From the Latin of Sannazarius

WRITTEN ON A WINDOW, IN THE HIGHLANDS OF SCOTLAND

Scotland! thy weather's like a modish wife!
Thy winds and ruins, forever are at strife:
So Termagant, a while, her Thunder tries,
And, when she can no longer scold – she cries.

Aaron Hill   *Works* (1753)

WRITTEN ON A CHIMNEY-PIECE,
AT THE GOLDEN BOAR'S HEAD
IN ROTTERDAM

Thro' this vile place, the signs in every street
Denote the filthy fore you're doomed to meet,
Here, the Swine's Head displays a brutal grin,
To mark the hog-sty you must find within
And shew, by gilded snout, so coldly carved
That through the nose you'll pay – for being starv'd.

An English Traveller 1793
Anon
A Collection of Poems, Epigrams etc. extracted From Newspapers
(1770–95?)

Ireland never was contented.
Say you so? You are demented.
Ireland was contented when
All could use the sword and pen,
And when Tara rose so high
That her turrets split the sky,
And about her courts were seen
Liveried angels robed in green,
Wearing, by St Patrick's bounty,
Emeralds big as half the county.

Walter Savage Landor   *Last Fruit* (1853)

BUNGALOID GROWTH

When England's multitudes observed with frowns
   That those who came before had spoiled the towns,
'This can no longer be endured!' they cried,
   And set to work to spoil the countryside.

Colin Ellis   *Mournful Numbers* (1932)

SNAPSHOT OF NAIROBI

With orange-peels the streets are strown
And pips, beyond computing,
On every shoulder save my own
That's fractured with saluting.

Roy Campbell   *Talking Bronco* (1946)

You ask me where I am going? Well,
I'm either passing through Italy on my way to Hell,
Or, to put the matter a bit too wittily
Passing through Hell on my way to Italy.

George Barker   *Villa Stellar* (1978)

UNCLASSIFIED

OF SIGHT

Who needs will look, and would not see,
The sight once seen thou lookest for,
Close up thine eyes. For, trust thou me,
Much looking so, breedeth much eye sore.

John Heywood   *An Hundred Epigrams* (1550)

TO ORESTES PREPARING TO KILL
HIS MOTHER

Where shorst thou in thy sword? through panch,
   or pap so tender soft?
The belly bred and brought thee forth,
   The pap did feed thee oft.

Timothe Kendall   *Flowres of Epigrammes* (1577)
From the Greek

Such was my grief upon my fatal fall
That all the world me thought was dark withal
And yet I was deceived as I know.
For when I prov'd I found it nothing so.
I shewd the Sun my lamentable sore,
The Sun did see and shined as before.
Then to the Moon I did reveal my plight,
She did diminish nothing of her light.
Then to the stars I went and let them see,
No not a star would shine the less for me.
Go wretched man, thou seest thou art forlorn
Thou seest the heavens laugh while thou dost mourn.

Thomas Bastard   *Chrestoleros* (1598)

OF PLENTY AND FREEDOM IN GOODNESS

Not to have want, what riches doth exceed?
Not to be subject, what superior thing?
He that to naught aspires, doth nothing need : *Resp.*
Who breaks no law, is Subject to no King.

George Chapman   *Petrarch's Seven Penitential Psalms* (1612)

NARCISSUS

Floods cannot quench my Flames, ah! in this well
I burn, not drown, for what I cannot tell.

William Drummond   *Poems Upon Various Subjects* (1616)

A RULE TO PLAY

Lay down your stake at play, lay down your passion:
A greedy gamester still hath some mis-hap.
To chafe at luck proceeds of foolish fashion.
No man throws still the dice in fortune's lap.

Sir John Harington
The Most Elegant and Wittie Epigrams (1618)

OF TREASON

Treason doth never prosper, what's the reason?
For if it prosper, none dare call it Treason.

Sir John Harington
The Most Elegant and Wittie Epigrams (1618)

PEACE AND WARS

Weapons in peace grow hungry, and will eat
Themselves with rust: but War allows them meat.

Thomas Bancroft
Two Books of Epigrammes and Epitaphs (1639)

ON WOMEN'S INCONSTANCY

Go catch a star that's falling from the sky,
Cause an immortal creature for to die,
Stop with thy hand the current of the seas,
Post o're the earth to the Antipodes,
Cause times return and call back yesterday;
Clothe January with the month of May,
Weigh out an ounce of flame, blow back the wind
And then find faith within a woman's mind.

Anon *Witt's Recreations* (1640)

DREAMS

Here we are all, by day; By night w'are hurl'd
By dreams, each one, into a sev'ral world.

Robert Herrick *Hesperides* (1648)

ON GELLIA

That you are black, Gellia, they falsely say;
Thou are blood-red, taking the skin away.

James Wright *Sales Epigrammatum* (1663)
From the Latin of Stephanus Ritterus

A WILD PARTRIDGE

I a wild Partridge am; what difference? nought,
But that the tame one is dearer bought.

James Wright *Sales Epigrammatum* (1663)
From the Latin of Martial

ON A SOW THAT FARROW'D THROUGH
A WOUND SHE RECEIV'D

I'th' publick Huntings Caesar did allow,
A Jav'lin swift transfixt a pregnant Sow.
Straight from the wounded Dam the Litter sprung.
Lucina, call'st thou this, to bring forth Young?
The dying Sow wish'd that her wounds were more,
That Issues had been made for all her Store.
Who denies *Bacchus* from the womb was torn?
A God might well, when Beasts were this way born.

Henry Killigrew *Epigrams of Martial, Englished* (1695)
From the Latin of Martial

THE LADY WHO OFFERS HER
LOOKING-GLASS TO VENUS

Venus, take my Votive Glass:
  Since I am not what I was;
What from this Day I shall be,
Venus, let Me never see.

Matthew Prior *Poems on Several Occasions* (1718)

ON A FEMALE ROPE DANCER

Whilst in her Prime, and Bloom of Years,
    Fair Celia trips the Rope;
Alternately she moves our Fears;
    Alternately our Hope.

But when she sinks, or rises higher
    Or graceful does advance;
We know not which we most admire,
    The Dancer, or the Dance.

Anon   *The Honey Suckle* (1734)

FLATTERY

It is a maxim in the schools,
That flattery is the food of fools;
But now and then your men of wit
Will condescend to take a bit.

Jonathan Swift
written c. 1740(?) Cheale, *Epigrams and Epitaphs* (1877)

WROTE AT THE REQUEST OF DR COX, ON A FAVOURITE LADY WHOM HE CALLED CHUBBY

Sally, Doctor Cox's Chubby,
Is nought but Belly, Bum and Bubby.

Anon   *The Nut Cracker* (1751)

IN POMPEIOS

Great Pompey's ashes, in vile Egypt lie;
His sons, in Europe, and in Asia, die:
What wonder, that these three, so distant, died,
So vast a ruin could not spread less wide!

Aaron Hill   Works (1753)

What would I do, the question you repeat
If on a sudden I were rich and great?
Who can himself with future conduct charge?
What would you do, a lion, and at large?

William Hay   Select Epigrams of Martial (1755)
From the Latin of Martial

ANCIENT AND MODERN
JUDAISM CONTRASTED

Old Jacob's sons, in ancient writ, we read
  Who to the Pit their Brother Joseph spurn'd,
Seem'd to repent of th' outrageous deed;
  They sold his Body, and his Coat return'd:-
But modern Jews have souls not quite so nice;
  For should a tribe of Ishmaelites come hither,
They'd add another talent to his price,
  And sell a Joseph and his coat together!

Anon   A Collection of Poems, Epigrams, etc.
Extracted from Newspapers (1770?–95?)

ON GRACE

Short is the triumph of that face,
Where beauty shines devoid of grace,
Fish may with joy the bait survey,
The hook alone secures the prey.

Anon   *Epigrams Translated Into English Verse* (1789)
From the Greek of Capito

SOFT SNOW

I walked abroad in a snowy day.
I asked the soft snow with me to play.
She played & she melted in all her prime
And the winter called it a dreadful crime.

William Blake   *Notebook &c.* 1793

ON MRS ROACH'S BEING DELIVERED OF TWIN SONS

For three successive nights poor Jonah lay
In belly of a whale, pent up at sea —
A wonder rare! — but sure it can't approach
To two fine boys — pent nine months in a Roach.

Anon   *The Spirit of the Public Journals for 1806*

ON A BEE HAVING STUNG THE
THIGH OF AN OLD MAID

In the annals of fame with Columbus you stand,
  Who first found the American shore
Advent'rous, like him, you explore a new land,
  Which by man unexplor'd was before.

                              Anon   *The Merry Fellow* (1811)

No charm can stay, no medicine can assuage,
The sad incurable disease of age;
Only the hand in youth more warmly prest
Makes soft the couch and calms the final rest.

                    Walter Savage Landor   *Works* (1846)

  Funny – to be a Century –
  And see the People – going by –
  I – should die of the Oddity –
  But then – I'm not so staid – as He –

  He Keeps His Secrets safely – very –
  Were He to tell – extremely sorry
  This Bashful Globe of Ours would be –
  So dainty of Publicity –

                    Emily Dickinson   written c. 1862
                    Further Poems of Emily Dickinson (1929)

THE TELESCOPE

Seemeth it strange that God should make
A star so distant for the sake
Of men whose unassisted sight
Cannot discern its twinkling light?
Do they not thus the scheme fulfil
Of imaging their Maker's skill,
When toward the heavenly vault they rear
The engine that can bring it near?

Anon   *Epigrams Sacred & Moral* (1864)

GOOD LUCK AND BAD

Good Luck is the gayest of all gay girls;
   Long in one place she will not stay:
Back from your brow she strokes the curls,
   Kisses you quick and flies away.

But Madame Bad Luck soberly comes
   And stays – no fancy has she for flitting, –
Snatches of true-love songs she hums,
   And sits by your bed, and brings her knitting.

John Milton Hay   *Complete Poetical Works* (1917)

RELATIVITY

I like relativity and quantum theories
because I don't understand them
and they make me feel as if space shifted about like a
swan that can't settle,
refusing to sit still and be measured;
and as if the atom were an impulsive thing
always changing its mind.

> D. H. Lawrence   *Pansies* (1929)

HAPPINESS

Happiness is silent, or speaks equivocally for friends,
Grief is explicit and her song never ends,
Happiness is like England, and will not state the case,
Grief like Guilt rushes in and talks apace.

> Stevie Smith   *Mother, What is Man?* (1942)

Ghost cries out to ghost –
But who's afraid of that?
I fear those shadows most
That start from my own feet.

> Theodore Roethke   *Words for the Wind* (1958)

from

A CHEERFUL ALPHABET OF
PLEASANT OBJECTS

APPLE

Since Time began, such alphabets begin
With Apple, source of Knowledge and of Sin.
My child, take heart : the fruit that undid Man,
Brought out as well the best in Paul Cézanne.

John Updike   *Verse* (1965)

To the man-in-the-street who I'm sorry to say,
    Is a keen observer of life,
The word *intellectual* suggests right away
    A man who's untrue to his wife.

W. H. Auden   *Collected Shorter Poems 1927–57* (1966)

THE DREAM OF FLYING COMES OF AGE

Remember those wingovers and loops and spins?
Forbidden. Heavy, powerful and solemn,
Our scheduled transports keep the straight and level.
It's not the joysticks now but the control column.

Howard Nemerov   *The Blue Swallows* (1967)

ON A SUNDIAL

I am a Sundial. Ordinary words
Cannot express my thoughts on Birds.

Hilaire Belloc   *Complete Verse* (1970)

THE LAST LAUGH

I made hay while the sun shone.
  My work sold.
Now, if the harvest is over
  And the world cold,
Give me the bonus of laughter
  As I lose hold.

John Betjeman   *A Nip in the Air* (1974)

Man stole fire, and Zeus created flame
much fiercer still. Woman was its name.

Fire's soon put out, but women blaze
like volcanic conflagration all our days.

Tony Harrison   *Palladas : Poems* (1975)
After the Greek of Palladas

Never in any circumstance
Let them induce you to refute.
Wise men fall into ignorance
When with the ignorant they dispute.

Michael Hamburger   *Goethe: Poems and Epigrams* (1983)
From the German of Goethe

BIBLIOGRAPHY

The books listed here represent only a fraction of the books consulted while preparing the anthology. This bibliography is being published as an aid to those who might wish to read epigrams at the source. It is, to the best of my knowledge, the most extensive bibliography of English verse epigram volumes ever prepared. In addition the works of all the major and minor poets should be consulted. There are also several eighteenth-century miscellanies in which scattered epigrams may be found: the *New Cambridge Bibliography of English Literature* contains a fairly comprehensive list of these. Back numbers of *Notes and Queries* and *Gentleman's Magazine* are another valuable source of stray epigrams.

COLLECTIONS OF EPIGRAPHS

I. INDIVIDUAL

CROWLEY Robert   *One and Thirty Epigrammes*   Holburne 1550
HEYWOOD John   *An Hundred Epigrammes*   1550
HEYWOOD John   *Two Hundred Epigrammes*   1555
HEYWOOD John   *A Fourth Hundred of Epigrams*   1560
HEYWOOD John   *John Heywoodes Workes . . . and a fifth hundred of epigrams; whereunto are now early added a syxt hundred of epigrams*   1562
TUBERVILLE George   *Epithaphes, Epigrams, Songs and Sonets*   1567
KENDALL Timothe   *Flowres of Epigrammes out of Sundrie the Most Singular Authors*   1577
DAVIES Sir John   *Epigrammes and Elegies*   159–?
GUILPIN Everard   *Skialetheia: or a shadow of truth in certain epigrams and satyres*   1598
BASTARD Thomas   *Chrestoleros: Seven books of epigrames*   1598

WEEVER John   *Epigrammes in the Oldest Cut, and Newest Fashion*   1599

GODDARD William   *A Mastif Whelp*   1599

THYNNE Francis   *Emblemes and Epigrames*   1600

COOKE John   *Epigrames, Served out in 52 Several Dishes*   c.1604

PARROT Henry   *The Mous-Trap*   1606

TURNER Richard   *Nosce Te*   1607

MIDDLETON Richard   *Epigrams And Satyres*   1608

PARROT Henry   *Epigrams*   1608

ROWLANDS Samuel   *Humours Looking Glasse*   1608

WEST Richard   *Wits ABC*   1608

PEACHAM Henry   *The More the Merrier*   1608

SHARPE Roger   *More Fooles Yet*   1610

HEATH John   *Two Centuries of Epigrames*   1610

DAVIES OF HEREFORD John   *The Scourge of Folly*   1611

DAVIES OF HEREFORD John   *Descant upon English Proverbes*   1611

TAYLOR John   *The Sculler: Rowing From Tiber to Thames With His Boate laden With a Hotch-Potch, or Gallimewfry of Sonnets, Satyres and Epigram*   1612

PARROT Henry   *Laquei Ridiculosi: or Springes for Woodcocks*   1613

WITHER George   *Abuses Stript and Whipt*   1613

GAMAGE William   *Linsi-Woolsie: or two centuries of epigrams*   Oxford 1613

NICCOLS Richard   *The Furies*   1614

FREEMAN Thomas   *Rubbe and a great cast: epigrams*   1614

PARROT Henry   *The Mastive or young-whelpe of old-dogge*   1615

GODDARD William   *A Neaste of Waspes*   Printed in the Low Countries   1615

BRATHWAITE Richard   *A Strappado for the Divell: Epigrams and Satyrs*   1615

JONSON Ben   *Epigrammes* entered in the Stationers Register, 15 May 1612

First pub. in *Workes*   1616

DRUMMOND William of Hawthornden   *Poems upon Various Subjects*   Edinburgh   1616

DAVIES OF HEREFORD John   *Wit's Bedlam*   1617

FITZGEFFREY Henry   *Satyres and Satiricall Epigrams*   1617

HARINGTON Sir John   *The Most Elegant and Wittie Epigrams &c*   1618

VICARS John   *Epigrams of That Most Wittie and Worthy Epigrammatist Mr John Owen*   1619

HEATH John   *The House of Correction*   1619

HUTTON Henry   *Follie's Anatomie*   1619

WROTE Thomas   *The Abortive of an Idle Houre*   1620

PEACHAM Henry   *Thalia's Banquet Furnished With an Hundred and Odde Dishes of Newly Devised Epigrammes*   1620

MARTYN Joseph   *New Epigrams and a Satyre*   1621

ASHMORE John   *Certaine selected odes of Horace, Englished . . . whereunto are added, both in Latin and English, Sundry new epigrammes, anagrams, epitaphs*   1621

PENKETHMAN John   *The Epigrams of P. Virgilius Maro*   1624

PARROT Henry   *Cures for the Itch*   1626

PYNE John   *Epigrammata Officiosa, Religiosa, Iocosa*   1627

HAYMAN Robert   *Quodlibets lately come over from new Britaniola*   1628

MAY Thomas   *Selected Epigrams of Martial*   1629

QUARLES Francis   *Divine Fancies*   1632

MAY Edward   *Epigrams Divine and Morall*   1633

ANON   *Epigrammes, Mirrour of New Reformation* (Also at Rouen before 1634)   Paris 1634

QUARLES Francis   *Emblemes*   1635

HEYWOOD Thomas   *Pleasant Dialogues and Drammas*   1637

CHAMBERLAIN Robert   *Nocturnal Lucubrations; whereunto are added epigrams and epitaphs*   1638

BANCROFT Thomas   *Two Books of Epigrammes and Epitaphs*   1639

JONSON Ben   *Execration against Vulcan.* With divers Epigrams   1640

URQUHART Sir Thomas   *Epigrams: Divine and Moral*   1641

PRYNNE WILLIAM   *A Pleasant Purge for a Roman Catholike to Evacuate His Evil Humours*   1642

HERRICK Robert   *Hesperides* (with *His Noble Numbers*)   1648

BARON Robert   *Pocula Castalia*   1650

HEATH Robert   *Clarastella*   1650

SHERBURNE Edward   *Salmacis*   1651

SHEPPARD Samuel   *Epigrams, Theological, Philosophical, Romantick*   1651

TAYLOR John   *Epigrammes*   1651

DELAUNE Henry   *ΠΑΤΡΙΚΟΝ ΔΩΡΟΝ*   1651

MAYNE Jasper   *Paradoxes, Problems, Essayes . . . written by Dr Donne . . . to which is added, a book of epigrams written in Latin by the same author etc.*   1652

ANON   *Ex Ungue Leonem*   1654

FLETCHER R.   *Ex Otio Negotium or Martial his Epigrammes translated*   1656

ELIOT John   *Poems: consisting of epistles and epigrams etc.*   1658

PECKE Thomas   *Parnassi Puerperium*   1659

HOLYDAY Barten   *A Survey of the World*   1661

WATKYNS Rowland   *Flamma Sine Fumo*   1662

COKAIN Aston   *Small Poems of Divers Sorts*   1662

WRIGHT James   *Sales Epigrammatum*   1663

BILLINGSLEY Nicholas   *Treasury of Divine Raptures consisting of Serious Observations, Pious Ejaculations, Select Epigrams . . .*   1667

FLECKNOE Richard   *A Collection of the Choicest Epigrams and Characters*   1673

FLECKNOE Richard   *Euterpe Revived*   1675

HARVEY Thomas   *John Owen's Latine Epigrams*   1677

BARKSDALE Clement   *Bezae Epitaphia Selecta cum anglica versione*   1680

BARKSDALE Clement   *Epigrammata sacra selecta, cum anglica versione*   1682

HODGKIN T. (?)   *Innocui Sales*   1694

KILLIGREW Henry   *A Book of New Epigrams*   1695

KILLIGREW Henry   *Epigrams of Martial, Englished*   1695

ELSUM John   *Epigrams upon the Paintings of the Most Eminent Masters, Ancient and Modern*   1700

MONTEITH Robert   *Three Books of Epigrams*   Edinburgh 1708

ANON   *Martial Reviv'd*   1725

ANON   *Epigrams in Distich*   1740

ANON   *Epigrams M S Binders' title*   (Newberry Library, Chicago) 1748?

DODD William   *The Hymns of Callimachus*   1755

HAY William   *Select Epigrams of Martial*   1755

NEWCOMB Thomas   *Novus Epigrammatium Delectus*   1760

PRICE of Cardiganshire   *Democritus: or The Laughing Philosopher*   1771?

SCOTT Revd   *Epigrams of Martial &c*   1773

ANON   *Theatrical portraits, epigramatically delineated*   1774

GRAVES Richard   *Euphrosyne or Amusements on the Road to Life*   1776

ANON   *Saint Stephen's tripod: or, Mother Shipton in the lower H**se*   1782

ELPHINSTON James   *The Epigrams of M. Vul. Martialis*   1782

ANON   *Caps well fit; or select epigrams, serious and comic*   Newcastle 1785

POLYWHELE Richard   *The Idyllia, Epigrams, and Fragments, of Theocritus, Bion, and Moschus*   1786

ANON   *Epigrams translated into English verse from the original Greek*   1789

ANON   *Epigrams, published for the benefit of Addenbrookes hospital on the fish convention, at T— college*   1790?

ANON   *A Selection of Greek Epigrams or Inscriptions from Brunck's Anthologia . . . for the use of Winchester School*   Oxford 1791

TYTLER H. W.   *The Works of Callimachus: The Hymns and Epigrams from the Greek*   1793

HALHED N. B.   *Immitations of some of the Epigrams of Martial* Parts I–IV   1793–4

BISHOP Samuel   *Poetical Works* Vol II   1796

WRANGHAM Francis (Signed 'X')   *Epigrams*   York? 1800?

NASH Samuel John   *Juvenile Epigrams*   Oxford 1800?

RHODES William Barnes   *Epigrams*   1803

BLAND R. & MERIVALE J. H.   *Translations Chiefly from the Greek Anthology*   1806

PYE Henry James   *A Translation of the Epigrams and Hymns of Homer*   1810

DUNBAR Thomas   *The Epigrammatique Garlande*   1818

HUNT J. & H. L.   *Fables and Epigrams* from the German of Lessing   1825

SWINTON & AYTOUN E.   *Translations and Imitation of Epigrams of Martial*   1829

PULLEYN William   *Churchyard Gleanings and Epigrammatic Scraps*   1830

MACGREGOR Major R. C.   *Epitaphs from the Greek Anthology* (including *Christian Epigrams* translated by Miss M. A. Stodart)   1857?

ANON ('A.G.W.')   *Epigrams, Sacred and Moral*   1864

EGERTON-WARBURTON R. E. (pseud. 'Rambling Richard')   *Epigrams and Humorous Verses* 1867

PURVES David Laing   *Epigrams and Literary Follies*   Edinburgh 1868

GARNETT Richard   *Idylls and Epigrams*   1869

ANON   *Epigrams and Other Short Excursions by a Cripple of Long Standing*   1869

LISTER John ('A.F.G.')   *Epigrams and Jeux D'Esprit*   1870

COLLINS W. L.   *The Greek Anthology*   1870

ROGERS J. E. Thorold   *Epistles, Satires and Epigrams*   1876

WARBURTON R. E. E.   *Poems, Epigrams and Sonnets*   1877

ANON   *Political Epigrams (1874–81)*   1881

BUTLER A. J.   *Amaranth and Asphodel*   1881

GUNNYON William   *A Century of translations from the Greek Anthology*   Kilmarnock 1883

WATSON William   *Epigrams of Art, Life and Nature*   Liverpool 1884

SNIDER Denton J.   *An Epigrammatic Voyage*   Boston 1886

HARFORD Fredrick Kill   *Epigrammatics Serious, Semiserious, and Divertive*   1890

BURTON Sir Richard   *Priapeia*   Cosmopolis 1890

ROUSE W. H. D.   *An Echo of Greek Song Englished*   1899

MORE Paul Elmer   *A Century of Indian Epigrams*   1899

HARDINGE William M.   *Chrysanthema*   1903

COBB G. H.   *Poems from the Greek Anthology*   1908

POTT J. A.   *Greek Love Songs and Epigrams*   1911

NIXON Paul   *A Roman Wit*   Boston 1911

GRUNDY G. B.   *Ancient Gems in Modern Settings*   1913

MELLOR C. W.   *Latin and English verse translations from the Greek Anthology*   Brighton 1914

BARNARD F. P.   *A Century of Epigrams* privately printed   1916

RODD Sir Rennell   *Love, Worship and Death*   1916

LEGGE J. G.   *Echoes from the Greek Anthology*   1919

LOTHIAN Alexander   *The Golden Treasury of the Greeks*   Oxford 1920

ALLISON Robert   *Translations into English Verse, Mainly from the Greek Anthology*   1921

LEAF Walter   *Little Poems from the Greek*   1922

BARNARD F. P.   *A Fardel of Epigrams*   1922

BENSON A. C.   *The Reed of Pan*   1922

LAWTON William Cranston   *The Soul of the Anthology*   New Haven 1923

WRIGHT F. A.   *The Girdle of Aphrodite*   1923

MACNAGHTEN Hugh   *Little Masterpieces From The Anthology*   Glasgow 1924

COLE Cornelius   *Ideals in Verse*   Los Angeles 1924

WOODWARD G. R.   *Collection of Poems from the Greek Anthology translated into English Verse*   1924

GUITERMAN Arthur   *A Poet's Progress*   New York 1924

236

WOLFE Humbert   *Lampoons*   1925

IBBETT William   *A Greek Garland of Amorous Trifles*   Shaftesbury 1925

MORLEY Christopher   *Epigrams in a Cellar*   Oxford 1927

WOLFE Humbert   *Others Abide*   1927

ANON   *Poems from the Greek* Augustan Books of English Poetry Ser.2 No. 8   1927

SOMERSET Henry Vere Fitzroy   *Half a Hundred Epigrams*   1928

LEWIS T. B.   *Translations from the Greek Anthology*   1929

LESLIE Shane   *The Greek Anthology*   1929

PHILLIPS Hubert   *A Diet of Crisps*   Oxford 1929

BABCOCK Mary Kent   *Owen's Epigrams and other echoes of Paris*   New York 1931

FURNESS R. A.   *Translations from the Greek Anthology*   1931

TAYLOR Geoffrey Basil   *A Dash of Garlic*   Warminster 1932

ANON   *Strato's Boyish Muse*   1932

ELLIS Colin   *Mournful Numbers; verses and epigrams*   1932

ARMSTRONG Martin   *54 Conceits*   1933

HAMILTON George Rostrevor   *Wit's Looking Glass*   1934

SOUTAR William   *Brief Words*   Edinburgh 1935

LUCAS F. L.   *The Golden Cockerel Greek Anthology*   1937

TAYLOR Geoffrey Basil   *Seven Simple Poems*   Sutton Very, Wilts. 1937

LUCAS F. L.   *A Greek Garland*   1939

MITCHELL David M.   *Translations from the Greek Anthology*   Letchworth 1940

REID Forrest   *Poems from the Greek Anthology*   1943

IRVINE John   *The Fountain of Hellas*   Belfast 1943

BLAIR Alan   *More Bright Brevities*   1944

HAMILTON George Rostrevor   *Selected Poems and Epigrams*   1945

GARROD Heathcote William   *Epigrams*   Oxford 1946

SACKVILLE Margaret   *Miniatures* (Second series)   Crayke, York   1956

DUDLEY Fitts   *Poems from the Greek Anthology* 2nd edn.   1956

SACKVILLE Margaret   *Quatrains and Other Poems*   Llandeilo 1960

REXROTH Kenneth   *Poems from the Greek Anthology*   1962

HUMPHRIES Rolph   *Selected Epigrams*   Bloomington, Indiana 1963

BEUM Robert   *Poems and Epigrams*   Chicago 1964

HEIN Piet   *Grooks*   Cambridge, Mass. 1966

FITTS Dudley   *Sixty Poems of Martial*   New York 1967

MURRAY Philip   *Poems after Martial*   Middletown, Conn. 1967
SINCLAIR Andrew   *Selection from the Greek Anthology*   1967
MARCELLINO Ralph   *Selected Epigrams*   Indianapolis 1968
HEATH-STUBBS John   *Satires and Epigrams*   1968
DAKIN Laurence   *Lyrics and Epigrams from the Greek Anthology*   1969
MILLS BARRIS   *Epigrams from Martial*   Lafayette, Indiana 1969
HEIN Piet   *More Grooks*   1969
LEFEVRE Andre   *Classical Epigrams. Love And Wit*   1970
HEIN Piet   *Still More Grooks*   1970
LUCIE SMITH Edward   *A Garland from the Greek*   1971
CUNNINGHAM J. V.   *Collected Poems and Epigrams*   1971
SKELTON Robin   *Two Hundred Poems from the Greek Anthology*   1971
HILL Brian   *Ganymede in Rome*   1971
HILL Brian   *An Eye for Ganymede*   1972
SPARROW John Hanbury A.   *Grave Epigrams*   Bembridge 1974
HARRISON Tony   *Palladas: Poems*   1975
WHIGHAM Peter   *The Poems of Meleager*   1975
PORTER Peter   *After Martial*   1976
O'CONNELL Richard   *Epigrams from Martial*   Van Nuys, Calif. 1976
MICHIE James   *Martial: The Epigrams*   1978
HARVEY Andrew   *Evidence*   1979
DAVENPORT Guy   *Archilochos, Sappho, Alkman*   Berkeley 1980
HARRISON Tony   *U. S. Martial*   1981
HAMBURGER Michael   *Goethe: Poems and Epigrams*   1983

II.   ANTHOLOGIES

ANON   *Witt's Recreations*   1640
ANON   *Recreation for Ingenious Head-pieces*   1654
OLDYS William (?)   *A Collection of Epigrams* 1727   2nd edn. 1735
ANON   *The London Medley: containing the Exercises spoken by several young Noblemen and Gentlemen at the Annual Meeting of the Westminster Scholars on the 28th of January 1730–1 at Westminster-School*   1731
ANON   *Certain Epigrams in Laud and Praise of the Gentlemen of the Dunciad*   1732
HACKETT John   *A Collection of Select Epigrams*   1757
GRAVES Richard   *The Festoon*   1766
ANON   *The Christmas treat: or gay companion*   Dublin 1767
RICKMANN Thomas Clio   *A Select Collection of Epigrams*   1796
DODD Philip S.   *Select Epigrams 2 Vols*   1797

ANON   *The British Martial* 2 Vols   1806

ANON   *Panorama of Wit*   1809

ANON   *A Selection of English Epigrams extracted principally from the British and American journals*   Boston 1812

KETT Revd Henry   *The Flowers of Wit*   1814

MUIRHEAD James Patrick   *Winged Words on Chantrey's Woodcocks*   1857

BOHN H. G.   *The Epigrams of Martial*   1860

BOOTH John   *Epigrams Ancient and Modern*   1863

REEVE Issac Jack   *The Wild Garland or Curiosities of Poetry* Vol II   1866

PALMER Samuel   *Epitaphs and epigrams, curious, quaint and amusing* 2nd edn.   1869

DODD H. P.   *The Epigrammatists*   1870

CAREY C. S.   *A Commonplace Book of Epigrams*   1872

TEGG W.   *Epitaphs and Epigrams*   1875

CHEALES Alan B.   *Epigrams and Epitaphs*   1877

STANDRING   *Epigrams: Original and Selected*   1877

ADAMS W. D.   *English Epigrams*   1879

ANON   *The Masque of B–ll—l*   Oxford 1881

ANON   *Epigram Evening November 5th 1888*   San Francisco 1888

ANON   *The Epigram Club Collection*   1891

STEWART Aubrey   *English Epigrams and Epitaphs*   1897

LEONARD R. M.   *Epigrams*   1915

JERROLD Walter Copeland   *Epigrams, Wit & Wisdom in Brief*   1926

OSBORN E. B.   *The Hundred Best Epigrams*   Oxford 1928

HAMILTON George Rostrevor   *The Soul of Wit*   1929

JAY Peter   *The Greek Anthology*   1973

GRIGSON Geoffrey   *The Faber Book of English Epigrams and Epitaphs*   1977

III.   COLLECTIONS CONTAINING EPIGRAMS

CAMPION Thomas   *Observations in the Art of English Poesie*   1602

PICK Samuel   *Festum Voluptatis*   1639

COTGRAVE John   *Wit's Interpreter, the English Parnassus*   1655

ANON   *Poems on Affairs of State* 4 Vols.   1703–7

FENTON   *Oxford and Cambridge Miscellany Poems*   1709

CAVENDISH William   *The charms of liberty . . . to which is added epigrams, poems and satyrs*   1709

WARD Edward (?)   *The Poetical Entertainer*   1712–3

HAMMOND *A New Miscellany of Original Poems, Translation and Imitations* 1729

ANON *The Scarborough Miscellany, for 1732, 1733, 1734* 1734

ANON *The Honey Suckle* 1734

MILLER Joe *Joe Miller's Jests; or, The Wits Vade-Mecum* 1739

ANON *The British Apollo* 3 vols. 4th edn. 1740

DODSLEY Robert *A Collection of Poems* 3 vols. 1748

FOOT Ferdinando *The Nut Cracker* 1751

BENNET Allen *Satirical Trifles* 1764

WARTON Thomas *The Oxford Sausage* 1764

QUIN James *Quin's Jests; or, the Facetious Man's Pocket-Companion* 1766

ANON *A genuine collection of the several pieces of political intelligence extraordinary, epigrams, poetry, &c.* 1766

ANON *The Patriotic Miscellany. Being a collection of interesting papers, jests, anecdotes, epigrams, &c, in the case of John Wilkes, Esq.* 1769

WHYTE Samuel *The Shamrock, or Hibernian Cresses* Dublin 1772

ANON *The Wits Miscellany* 1774

KNOX *Elegant Extracts – Poetry* 1784

ANON *The Arno Miscellany; being a collection of fugitive pieces written by the members of a Society called the Oziosi* Florence 1784

ANON *Garrick's Jests; or, Genius in High Glee* 1785

ANON *A Collection of Odes, Songs, and Epigrams, against the Whigs, alias the Blue and Buff* 1790

ANON *Shakespeare's jests, or the jubilee jester* (1790?)

ANON *Salmagundi* 1791

ANON *The Poetical Farrago* 1794

PAINE Tom & others *Tom Paine's Jests* 1794

ANON *A Collection of Poems, Epigrams etc. extracted from Newspapers 1770–95?* (British Museum 664m. 15) 1795

ANON *The Spirit of the Public Journals* for 1797 (– 1874, 1823, 1824, 1825) 1798–1826

ANON *The Merry Companion* 1811

ANON *Facetiae Cantabrigiensis* 1825

LEMON Mark *The Jest Book* 1864

HEBEL William & HUDDSON Hoyt *Poetry of the English Renaissance* New York 1929

REFERENCE WORKS ON EPIGRAMS

I. BOOKS AND DISSERTATIONS

CARICATO Frank S. *John Donne and the Epigram Tradition*
(unpublished Ph.D. dissertation Fordham Univ.) 1973

HAMILTON Sir George Rostrevor *English Verse Epigram* 1965

HUDSON Hoyt H. *Elizabethan and Jacobean Epigrams*
(unpublished dissertation Cornell Univ.) 1923

HUDSON Hoyt H. *The Epigram in the English Renaissance* Princeton
1947

HUME M. M. *Yeats: Aphorist and Epigrammatist: A Study of
Collected Poems* (unpublished Ph.D. dissertation Univ. of Colorado)
1969

HUMEZ Jean McMahon *The Manners of Epigrams: A Study of the
Epigram volumes of Martial, Harington and Jonson*
(unpublished Ph.D. dissertation Yale Univ.) 1971

LANGVARDT Arthur Leroy *The Verse Epigram in English during the
Sixteenth and Early Seventeenth Centuries*
(unpublished Ph.D. dissertation Univ. of Colorado) 1956

MOORE Charles Magee *Epigrammatic Art in English Poetry of the
Classical School* (unpublished Ph.D. dissertation Univ. of
Pennsylvania) 1905

NIXON Paul *Martial and the Modern Epigram* 1927

SPENCER Henry Allan *English Popular Epigrams in the Renaissance*
(unpublished Ph.D. dissertation Rochester Univ.) 1976

WHIPPLE Thomas K. *Martial and the English Epigram from Sir Thomas
Wyatt to Ben Jonson* (Univ. of California Publications in Modern
Philology Vol. 10) Berkeley 1925

II. ESSAYS AND ARTICLES

ANON 'A Gossip on Epigrams' *Sharpe's London Magazine* Vol. 10
1849

ANON 'Epigrams' *Blackwood's Edinburgh Magazine* Vol. 93 1863

ANON 'Epigrams' *Home and Foreign Review* Vol. 3 1863

ANON 'Epigrams' *Chamber's Journal* Vol. 19 Edinburgh 1863

ANON 'Epigrams' *North British Review* Vol. 47 1865

ANON 'A Lost Literary Art' *All the Year Round* Vol. 5 New
Series 1870

ANON 'The Art of Epigrams' *Chamber's Journal* Vol. 59 Edinburgh 1882

ANON 'The Anatomy of the Epigram' *Atlantic Monthly* Vol. 67 1890

ANON 'Epigrams, Kindly and Stinging' *Spectator* Vol. 67 1891

ANON 'The Use and Abuse of Epigram' *Spectator* Vol. 83 1899

ANON 'Epigram' *Encyclopaedia Britannica* 11th edn. 1910

ANON 'English Epigrams' *Times Literary Supplement* 8 March 1934

ATKINS Sidney 'Certain of Sir Thomas More's Epigrams Translated By Stanihurst' *Modern Language Review* Vol. 26 1931

ATKINS Sidney 'Thomas Bastard' *Times Literary Supplement* 26 Sept. 1936

BOWYER William (trans.) 'Of Epigram' in Joseph Trapp's *Lectures on Poetry* (translated from *Praelectiones Poeticae* 3 Vols. 1711, 1715, 1719) 1742

COLLINS Mortimer 'An Essay on Epigrams' *Belgravia* Vol. 14 1871

COWAN W. 'Some Ancient and Modern Epigrams' *Good Words* Vol. 34 1893

CUNNINGHAM J. V. (trans.) Pierre Nicole's 'Essay on true and apparent beauty in which from settled principles is rendered the grounds for choosing and rejecting epigrams'. (Introduction to *Epigrammation Delectus* 1659)

DAVIES James 'Epigrammatists and Epigrams' *Contemporary Review* Vol. 14 1870

DAVIES James 'Epigrams' *Quarterly Review* Vol. 117 1865

DODD H. P. Introduction to *The Epigrammatists* 1870

ENNIS Lambert 'Wits Bedlam of John Davies of Hereford' *Huntingdon Library Bulletin* No. 11 1937

FOWLER Alistair 'Short sharp and to the point' *Times Literary Supplement* 23 Dec. 1977

GOSSE Edmund 'Seventeenth Century Epigrams' *Harpers Magazine* Vol. 112 1905

GRAVES 'An Essay on the Nature of the Epigram' *Euphrosyne* 1776

HELLEMS F. B. R. 'The Epigram and its Greatest Master' *Univ. of Colorado Studies* Vol. 4 1906

HUDSON Hoyt H. 'Edward May's Borrowings from Timothe Kendall and Others'. *Huntington Library Bulletin* No. 11 1937

HUDSON Hoyt H. 'Grimald's Translations from Beza' *Modern Language Notes* Vol. 39 1924

HUNT J. & H. L. (trans.)   Lessing's 'Essay on Epigram' in *Fables and Epigrams* From the German of Lessing   1825

LEE USTICK W. and HUDSON Hoyt H.   'Wit, "Mixt Wit," and the Bee in Amber' *Huntington Library Bulletin* No. 8   1935

MATTHEWS Brander   'American Epigrams' *Harpers Monthly Magazine* Vol. 107   New York 1903

MILLIGAN Burton A.   'Humor and Satire in Heywoods Epigrams' Allen, *Studies in Honor of T. W. Baldwin*, Urbana,   Illinois 1950

NEWCOMB Robert   'Poor Richard and the English Epigram' *Philological Quarterly*   Iowa City 1961

PITMAN Margaret C.   'The Epigrams of Henry Peacham and Henry Parrot'   *Modern Language Review* Vol. 29   1934

ROLL Hyder E.   'Samuel Pick's Borrowings' RES Vol. 7   1931

SMITH Philip A.   'Notes on Elizabethan and Jacobean Epigrams' *Faculty Papers of Union College* Vol. 2

WILLIAMS Franklin B.   'Henry Parrot's Stolen Feathers' *PMLA* Vol. 52

WILLIAMS Franklin B.   'The Epigrams of Henry Parrot' *Harvard Studies and Notes in Philology and Literature* Vol. 20   1938

WORDSWORTH William   'Essays Upon Epitaphs I, II, III' (see Owen, *Wordsworth's Literary Criticism* 1974)

ACKNOWLEDGEMENTS

An anthology owes a special debt to librarians. For all the assistance I have received I would like to thank the librarians of the Arts Council Poetry Library, London; the Asiatic Society, Bombay; the Bodleian, Oxford; the British Council Library, Bombay; the Columbia University Library, New York; the New York Public Library; Trinity College, Cambridge; the University of Bombay and in particular the staff and librarians of the North Library and Reading Room at the British Museum where most of my reading was done.

The extended kindness of friends saved me from the horrors of boarding houses and made the entire project possible. For their hospitality I am grateful to:

In London: Suzanna Taverne and Adrian Zuckerman; Edward St Aubyn and Rachel Astor; Charity and Tim Broadbent; Paul Palley; Martin Smith; Peter Giffen; Arti and Shibcharan Singh.

In Oxford: Paul Taylor and Susan Cleave; Sudhir Anand; Adrian Zuckerman.

In Cambridge: Rowan Moore.

In New York: Paul and Ann Grand.

In Bombay I have to thank P. S. and Leela Baboo for letting me use their vacant flat as an office.

It would be difficult to list the number of people I have spoken to on the subject of English epigrams but I have profited most from discussions with Alistair Fowler, Roger Lonsdale, Paul Taylor and David Ricks.

My thanks also to:

Tom Chandos for *Epitaph for Oscar Wilde*, the only epigram in the book that derives from an oral source.

Catherine Koralek and Scheherazade Daneshkhu for checking

and re-checking details in English libraries while I was in India. Felicia Fernandez, Padmini Bhatia and my parents for helping me compile the index.

Felicia Fernandez and Clarissa Carvalho for spending the best part of a Bombay winter typing out the contents of the several thousand file cards on which I had scrawled epigrams and then preparing a typescript for the publishers.

David Kewley and Sonny Mehta at Pan Books for all their patience and encouragement.

My parents and Scheherazade Daneshkhu for everything else.

The publishers would like to thank the following for permission to reproduce material:

'Ald Port . . .' From *A Look Around the Estate* by Kingsley Amis. © 1963 by Kingsley Amis. Reprinted by permission of Jonathan Cape Ltd. 'A Poet's Epitaph' from *A Case of Samples* by Kingsley Amis. Copyright © 1956 Kingsley Amis. Reprinted by permission of Jonathan Clowes Ltd, London, on behalf of Kingsley Amis. 'To a Jilt' and 'Reviewers' from *54 Conceits* by Martin Armstrong. Reprinted by permission of the Peters Fraser & Dunlop Group Ltd. 'When two persons discover', 'We've covered ground', 'Symmetries & Asymmetries', 'Epitaph for the Unknown Soldier', 'To the man-in-the-street', 'Whether determined by God' and 'Epitaph on a Tyrant' from *Collected Poems* by W. H. Auden, edited by Edward Mendelson. Reprinted by permission of Faber and Faber Limited. 'You ask me where I am going?' from *Villa Stellar* by George Barker. 'Mademoiselle Desirée lounges in front of me' from *In Memory of David Archer* by George Baker. Both reprinted by permission of Faber and Faber Limited. 'Gnome' from *Collected Poems 1930–1989* by Samuel Beckett. Copyright © The Samuel Beckett Estate 1992. Reprinted by permission of The Samuel Beckett Estate and Calder Publications Limited. 'On Lady Poltagrue', 'Epitaph on a Politician', 'On a Sundial', 'On a Puritan' and 'Lord Finchley' from *Complete Poems* by Hilaire Belloc. Published by Pimlico, a division of Random Century. Reprinted by permission of the Peters Fraser & Dunlop Group Ltd. 'The Last Laugh' from *A Nip in the Air* by John Betjeman. Reprinted by permission of John Murray (Publishers) Ltd. 'Poems for Spain' and 'Snapshot of Nairobi' from *Talking Bronco* by Roy Campbell. Reprinted by permission of Faber and Faber Limited. 'A Schoolmaster' from *Mithraic Emblems* by Roy Campbell. Reprinted by permission of Francisco Campbell Custodio and Ad. Donker (Pty) Ltd. 'Living on Sin' from *Collected Poems* by Austin Clarke. Reprinted by permission of R. Dardis Clarke, 21 Pleasants Street, Dublin 8. 'A Question of Values' from *Not Yet the Dodo* by Noël Coward. Copyright © by the Estate of Noël Coward. Reprinted by permission of Michael Imson Playwrights Ltd, 28 Almeida Street, London NI ITD. 'Mr Youse needn't be so spry' and 'red flag and pink flag' from *e. e. cummings' Selected Poems 1923–58* by e. e. cummings. Copyright © 1954 E. E. Cummings Trust. 'Fellow Sufferers' from *Singing as I Go* by Charles Dalman. Reprinted by permission of Constable Publishers. 'Where are our war poets?' from *World All Over* by Cecil Day Lewis and 'Epitaph for a drug addict' by Cecil Day Lewis. Reprinted by permission of Sinclair-Stevenson from *Complete Poems of C. D. Lewis* © 1992. 'Points of View' from *Collected Poems* by Walter de la Mare. Reprinted by permission of the Literary Trustees of Walter de la Mare and the Society of Authors as their representative. 'Glasgow Schoolboys, Running Backwards' from *Selected Poems 1964–1983* by Douglas Dunn. Reprinted by permission of Faber and Faber Limited. 'Piccadilly' from *Collected Poems 1931–1974* by Lawrence Durrell, edited by J. A. Brigham. Reprinted by permission of Faber and Faber Limited. 'The consolations of natural philosophy' from *My Country* by Alistair Elliot, published 1989. Reprinted by permission of Carcanet Press Limited. 'A Remarkable Thing' and 'Thought about the Human Race' from *All My Little Ones* by Gavin Ewart. Reprinted by

1948, 1962. 'To Posterity' and 'To a Communist' from *Collected Poems of Louis MacNeice*, edited by R. E. Dodds. Reprinted by permission of Faber and Faber Limited. 'The Impotent Lover' translated by W. S. Merwin from *The Greek Anthology* edited by Peter Jay. Reprinted by permission of Penguin Books Ltd. 'Fascist Speaker' and 'Remember Suez' from *For Beauty Douglas* by Adrian Mitchell. Reprinted by permission of the Peters Fraser and Dunlop Group Ltd. 'I wrote, she never' and 'Because he hates to praise by name' from *Martial: The Epigrams*. Copyright © 1978 by James Michie. 'Furious, your little villa' and 'I can remember, Lesbia' from *Catallus* by James Michie. Copyright © 1972 by James Michie. Reprinted by permission of James Michie. 'The dream of flying' from *The Blue Swallows* by Howard Nemerov. 'Power to the People' from *Gnomes and Occasions* by Howard Nemerov. 'Origin', 'Capitals', 'He' from *The Western Approaches* by Howard Nemerov. 'A Sacrificed Author' from *Collected Poems* by Howard Nemerov. 'A grain of salt' from *Inside the Onion* by Howard Nemerov. All Howard Nemerov poems reprinted by permission of Margaret Nemerov. 'The ambiguous fate' from *How do you withstand, body*, published by Clearing House, Calcutta. Reprinted by permission of Gieve Patel. 'Yours is a classic dilemma' and 'Sotades' head' from *After Martial* by Peter Porter. © Peter Porter 1972. Also in Peter Porter's *Collected Poems* (1983). 'Annotations from Auschwitz' from Peter Porter's *Collected Poems* (1983). Reprinted from Peter Porter's *Collected Poems* (1983) by permission of Oxford University Press. 'Homage to Quintus Septimus Florens Christianus, III: A sad and great evil' and 'Meditato' from *Collected Shorter Poems* by Ezra Pound. Reprinted by permission of Faber and Faber Limited.

'Academic' and 'A ghost comes out' from *Collected Poems of Theodore Roethke*. Reprinted by permission of Faber and Faber Limited. 'The bath-house bench' translated by W. G. Shepherd from *The Greek Anthology*, edited by Peter Jay. Reprinted by permission of Penguin Books Ltd. 'Happiness'

INDEX OF
EPIGRAMMATISTS

251

INDEX OF FIRST LINES

266